Alfred Bohner

Two on a Pilgrimage

The 88 Holy Places of Shikoku

Bohner, Alfred

Two on a Pilgrimage

The 88 Holy Places of Shikoku

Transcribed, edited and annotated by David C. Moreton.

Translated by Katharine Merrill.

1. Auflage 2011 | ISBN/EAN: 9783867417556

© Europäischer Hochschulverlag GmbH & Co KG, Fahrenheitstr. 1, 28359 Bremen. All rights reserved.

www.eh-verlag.de | office@eh-verlag.de

Alfred Bohner

Two on a Pilgrimage

The 88 Holy Places of Shikoku

Two on a Pilgrimage
The 88 Holy Places of Shikoku

By Alfred Bohner
Translated by Katharine Merrill

Transcribed, edited and annotated by David C. Moreton

Editor's Note:
About the title of the book

An important term related to the Shikoku pilgrimage is *dōgyō ninin* (two people, one practice), which means that a pilgrim does not make the lengthy and ardous pilgrimage around the island of Shikoku alone, but that Kukai/Kōbō Daishi (774-835), the founder of the Shingon sect of Buddhism in Japan and one of most well known and respected figures in Japanese history, travels with that pilgrim offering support, protection and comfort throughout the journey.

I believe that the title which Alfred Bohner used for his 1931 German book about this pilgrimage, namely *Wallfahrt zu Zweien*, which has been translated as "Two On A Pilgrimage" for the 1941 English edition, does not literally mean two people participating in the pilgrimage together, but is a translation of *dōgyō ninin*.

Preface

In 1999, I learned about the possible existence of an unpublished English translation of Alfred Bohner's book about the Shikoku pilgrimage, *Wallfahrt zu Zweien: Die 88 Heiligen Stätten von Shikoku* (1931), from a postscript note in Oliver Statler's *Japanese Pilgrimage* (1983) while I was a graduate student at the University of British Columbia in Vancouver, Canada.[1] However, at that time I was unable to attain this English edition, and asked some German friends to translate parts of of the German edition for use in my dissertation. I found it amazing that a Westerner had made the Shikoku pilgrimage as early as 1927 and had produced such a lengthy and comprehensive book about this topic.

Almost a decade later after seeing the reference in Statler's book I gave a talk in Japanese about Alfred Bohner at a pilgrimage conference in Japan. I was able to give this presentation about Bohner because I had received information from his daughter, Hanna Strauss Bohner (b.1923) who I was able to locate and correspond with frequently via letter for several years. There was a strong interest among the audience about Alfred Bohner and his book,

---

[1] Oliver Statler. Japanese Pilgrimage. Tuttle Publishing. Vermont, 1983. P.339. "…and on Alfred Bohner's Wallfahrt zu Zweien (Tokyo: German Society for the Study of the Countries and Peoples of East Asia, 1931) in an unpublished translation by Katharine Merrill Skog (1941)…".

2

and many people suggested two things: 1) that I republish the original German edition, which I was able to do in 2010; and 2) that I try to track down the English edtion and publish it. The only clues, however, I had of the unpublished translation was the name of Katharine Merrill (1895-1983)[2] in Statler's book, a little information about Bohner and Merrill from Hanna, and a line in the listing of the materials in the Oliver Statler Collection stored in the Special Collections at the Univeristy of Hawaii at Manao which states: "Alfred Bohner – Two On A Pilgrimage."

First of all, I asked a friend who lives in Hawaii to go the library on my behalf and look at the contents of this file. Once I saw the photographs he sent me, I realized that this was the English translation which Statler referred to. But why did Statler have a copy? How did he get it? I then requested the university to scan the entire unbound typed manuscript and send it to me. On the page entitled, "Translator's Note of the English edition," I discovered that Bohner and Merrill knew each other while they were working in Matsuyama city during the 1920s and that Bohner had asked Merrill to translate his book into English with "the hope that others will enjoy and profit by reading the book, and will thereby widen and deepen their

---

[2] For information on Katharine Merrill, see the following website at the Special Collections at Mount Holyoke College, US: http://www.mtholyoke.edu/lits/library/arch/col/msrg/mancol/ms0571r.htm

knowledge of Japan." In fact, Merrill and Bohner maintained their friendship for decades. But this information did not answer the question as to how Statler and Merrill met and how Statler obtained a copy of this English edition.

In the fall of 2010, I went to Hawaii to have a look at the Oliver Statler collection for clues to these questions. I was very fortunate to find several letters scattered throughout his materials, dated 1971 and 1972, between Statler and Merrill, which offered an answer. It seems that while Statler was making his pilgrimage around Shikoku in 1971, Merrill was visiting Matsuyama at the same time and they happened to meet a dinner party and talk about the pilgrimage. It can be assumed that Statler must have asked Merrill to lend him the English translation. She agreed to do this, but in a letter to Statler she noted that the original manuscript had been lost, and so she would have to send him a copy. After Statler read the manuscript he wrote Merrill, saying, "I enjoyed reading your translation of Dr. Bohner's book and I profited from it. It contains a wealth of materials about the pilgrimage. I think the most valuable part of the book is that where he relates his personal experiences...."[3] But before Statler returned the copy to Merrill, he made a copy of the copy and kept it in his

---

[3] letter by Oliver Statler dated January 2, 1972. University of Hawaii at Manoa. Oliver Statler Collection

4

collection. It is very fortunate that he did this because according to the relatives of Katharine Merrill, the original and copy that Katharine Merrill once had could no longer be found.

I would like to sincerely thank Sune Efolson, the eldest grandchild of Katharine Merrill, for giving me permission to republish this very significant English manuscript on the Shikoku pilgrimage.

David C. Moreton
http://www.davidmoreton.com

Introduction

Alfred Bohner was not the first documented Westerner to make the Shikoku pilgrimage, but he is the first one to write an extensive work about this topic and to include many rare photographs of the temples and pilgrims. Despite this achievement it is odd that although there are countless references in newspapers and books to Frederick Starr (1853-1933), the well-known University of Chicago anthropology professor who made the Shikoku pilgrimage in 1917 and 1921, there are only a few brief extent references to Alfred Bohner. For example, one such reference is found in a Japanese book from 1939 entitled, *Henro to Jinsei* (Pilgrim and Life) by Takamure Itsue (1894-1964) who wrote, "Among the foreigners [to make the Shikoku pilgrimage] there is the American Dr. Starr and the German, Alfred Bohner. He was formerly a teacher at Matsuyama high school and wrote a book entitled, 'Two on a Pilgrimage.'" [4] Forty-four years later, in 1983, Oliver Statler (1915-2002) makes four references to Bohner in *Japanese Pilgrimage*. For example, he stated that, "Bohner, a German, was teaching in Matsuyama; in 1927 he made the pilgrimage and wrote a book about it."[5] Then, in 2006, in the *Nanzan Guide to Japanese Religions*, an author wrote that, "In

---

[4] Takamure Itsue. *Henro to Jinsei.* (Tokyo: Koseikaku, 1939) 67.
[5] Oliver Statler, *Japanese Pilgrimage.* 229.

the West, Alfred Bohner published the first study of this pilgrimage in German in 1931."[6] Other than these sporadic, incidental comments about Alfred Bohner, his life, his experience in Japan, his pilgrimage, and the contents of his book have not been examined nor have they been accessible to the English reader. Allow me to offer a profile of Alfred given by his daughter Hanna, comments about him from former students, details about his pilgrimage contained within his book, and explain about the pilgrim attire he used.

[6] Barbara Ambros. "Geography, Environment, Pilgrimage." *Nanzan Guide to Japanese Religions.* (Honolulu: University Hawaii Press, 2006), 296.

Photo of Alfred Bohner from the Matsuyama school al-
bum[7]

---

[7] Matsuyama Dosokai ed., *Shashin-shu, Gyōun Komuru*. Matsuyama Kotogakko Soritsu 70shunen kinen, Matsuyama, 1990.
P122.

8

Profile:

Alfred Bohner was born on April 11, 1894, in Accra, Ghana, where his father, Heinrich Bohner, was stationed as a missionary of the Basler Mission, a Swiss evangelical organization. Alfred was the youngest of thirteen children and studied in Munich and Würzburg, Germany. During World War I, while he worked in Algiers as private teacher of a family, he was detained and spent four years as civilian POW in a prison camp in Corsica.

Around 1921, Alfred was unable to find work in Germany so he contacted his brother Hermann, who was living and teaching in Japan, and asked about possible employment there.[8] As a result, Hermann was able to find him a position starting in the spring of 1922 at Matsuyama High School in Matsuyama city, Japan to teach German and music. Alfred gladly accepted the job offer, but he did not want to go by himself so on May 12, 1921 he got mar-

---

[8] Hermann Bohner (1884-1963), served in the German navy during World War I and was captured by the Japanese in China and confined for five years in POW camps, first in Matsuyama (Ehime prefecture), then in Bando (Naruto-city, Tokushima prefecture). After the war he stayed in Japan and taught at various schools, for example, the Osaka University of Foreign Studies, until his death in 1963. He is buried in Kobe. Hermann published many papers on Japanese subjects. A brochure with the title "Hermann Bohner – Arbeiten und Veröffentlichungen betreffend Ostasien" (Papers and publications concerning East Asia, 52 pages) published by the Osaka University of Foreign Studies in 1955, lists his writings.

ried and later traveled to Japan with his wife, Cornelia. Approximately a year after their arrival, on July 6, 1923, their daughter Hanna was born.[9] During their stay, Alfred also taught at the Cadet Marine Academy in Hiroshima, but due to his work schedule, his wife was often left alone and didn't adjust very well to the Japanese life and climate. Therefore in late 1926, Alfred took Cornelia and Hanna back to Germany via the Trans-Siberian Railway and arrived in Germany at the beginning of 1927. Alfred returned to Japan by himself to work until the end of his contract, but between July and August 1927 he embarked on the Shikoku pilgrimage and by using trains and cars completed the entire journey in three weeks.

In the fall of 1927, Alfred gave a speech on the Shikoku pilgrimage in Tokyo at the German Society for Natural Science and Ethnology of East Asia. The audience found his story very interesting and suggested that he publish his experiences and research. Bohner extended the text, including further background material, and published

---

[9] Alfred and Cornelia had two other children: Hedwig (b.1929) and Hermann (b.1935). Hanna is the only one of the three children who has ever been in Japan. She had planned to visit Japan in 1983 with her cousin Heinrich, but an illness prevented her to go. Heinrich is the son of Gottlob (1888-1963), an older brother of Alfred, who spent three years in Japan from 1925 to 1928, teaching in Kochi prefecture on the island of Shikoku. In 1927, Gottlob wrote a book, *Ein Jahr in Japan*, which describes his experiences during that year. He briefly mentions the Shikoku pilgrimage and pilgrims that he saw at the temple near his home.

it in Tokyo in 1931 under the title "Wallfahrt zu Zweien – die 88 heiligen Stätten von Shikoku."[10] An advertisement from 1930 describes the German edition and its contents:

> This work is the first attempt to give a scientific description of the pilgrimage life that still today has a relevant role in the Japanese popular life. The "88 Sacred Sites of Shikoku" are situated on a 1200 kilometer long pilgrimage route, that has been entirely covered by the writer as the first European in 1927, sharing the pilgrim's simple food and rest places at temples and inns…. The book is divided into four parts, an historical one and three descriptive ones….A precious addition to the book are the numerous photographs taken by the author, an appendix and a comprehensive bibliography."

In March 1928, Alfred returned to Germany and gave several talks about Japan and Shikoku. Twelve years later, he submitted his book to the University of Bonn as his dissertation for a doctoral degree. During World War II, he served in the German Air-force as a military interpreter and dealt with English and French speaking prisoners. He

---

[10] Republished in 2010 by Europäischer Hochschulverlag, Germany.

describes some of his wartime experiences in a letter to Katharine Merrill dated November 3rd, 1946: "From 1941 onwards, I became Head of the Department of evaluation and appreciation of captured Air Force documents…After being captured by the French on April 21, 1945; I was later handed over to the Americans, and then flown to England for interrogation." Bohner eventually spent ten months in captivity – in England, Belgium and Munster, Germany - and was released on May 31st, 1946. Unfortunately, when he was captured, all of his possessions including his collection of Japanese scrolls and materials about Japan, Shikoku and the pilgrimage were seized and never returned.[11] After the war Alfred tried to reclaim his confiscated materials, but was unsuccessful. After being freed as a POW he returned to his teaching position at the school he had previously taught at in Germany. Until his death in 1954, Bohner remained strongly interested in Japan.

As a teacher:

Alfred spent six years living and teaching in Japan, but descriptions about him by other people are sparse.

---

[11] According to Hanna, "Alfred had probably written a diary while he was on the pilgrimage trail, which he later used when writing his book, but this and twice the amount of photographs that appear in this book, ie, possible photographs of him as a pilgrim, were taken away when he was detained as a POW." Email: November 23, 2006.

Fortunately, however, some former students wrote about him in letters they submitted to the school he taught at in Matsuyama.[12]

Here are the comments of three students:

1. Bohner was very open-hearted and easy to approach.... He lived in a house very close to the school and would take off his shoes because there were tatami rooms. He laughed and said that the Western custom of entering a room with shoes on was dirty.... During the summer he spent time in Ashiya.[13]

2. The German Bohner thought of various ideas for his classes. A sports day was held and even though Bohner was a little chubby, he made it around the track without giving up. I thought, 'That is a German for you.' He said that during World War I he became a prisoner of war.... He was a very diligent teacher. He bought and read the government authorized textbooks. Slowly his [Japanese] reading ability increased.

3. The German folk songs he sang were beautiful.... His rudimental Japanese was quite memorable, but when I met Bohner he had gotten quite used to Japanese and was always walking about campus reading a book.... When we were students, he went back to Germany once

---

[12] Matsuyama Kotogakko Dosokai. ed. *Matsuyama Kotogakko Soritsu 65nen shunen kinen. Shinzenbi.* (Matsuyama: Kanyo-kamiten, 1984)

[13] His brother Hermann Bohner lived in Ashiya.

for a break. At that time an article appeared in the Nankai Shimbun with his leaving words written in an eloquent matter, which he wrote himself…. The true self of Bohner that we saw showed a true talent for teaching his native language, German…. There are very few people who have a special talent to teach their own language and I never met another teacher like him during the rest of my life.

As a pilgrim:

Bohner's confiscated pilgrimage diary and photographs could have provided a lot more information regarding his journey around Shikoku. So, it is unfortunate that the only few clues can be found within his published book or from his family. For example, in regards to when and how he made the pilgrimage, he wrote that he "visited the temples around Matsuyama in two days and the remaining between 12 July and 5 August, 1927. And in between I came back to Matsuyama for four days. Without that visit the trip would have taken 23-24 days." (p. 200) Another time, he mentioned that he was a "pilgrim travelling luxuriously by train and auto" (p. 181) as it would be impossible to complete the 1,200 kilometer journey in about three weeks just by walking.

Bohner also recorded many unforgettable moments in his book. For example, one time "…when I was at temple I was repeatedly given beer at breakfast because it is written in junior high school textbooks that beer replaces tea in Germany." (p. 213) Another time he forgot a kimono for bathing and rice-bowl for eating and had to sleep on stiff futons. He also wrote that there were few guests at the low quality inns he stayed at, but one day he had a bad experience. He noted "the desire to continue the journey left me for several hours when one morning after leaving one such inn I discovered a well-nourished body-louse on my small Japanese towel." (p. 211)

Bohner also mentioned that he was greatly impressed with the custom of hospitality and often received gifts and assistance from others along the pilgrimage route. He explained that this charitiable act is something "not dreamed of in modern cities, even in Japan. And this has been going on for centuries!" (p. 37) He later added that:

> This beautiful custom is naturally born from the same spirit as the Word of Christ teaches us: 'What you do the least of my brothers, you do to me.' He who feeds the pilgrims, feeds the Daishi who makes the journey with him; in some places a local housewife brings two bowls with rice, one for us and one for our invisible companion. Also there are people along the pilgrimage route who, in the spring, tidy their best room and make it a resting place for pilgrims. (p. 185)

Pilgrim Attire:

According to Hanna, it seems that Bohner did not talk much about the Shikoku pilgrimage with his family, but she does remember that her father said that during his pilgrimage he attempted *takuhatsu* (begging) and took the white vest, staff, sedge hat and bag back to Germany. In his book he states that, "I had not once put on the pilgrim garments, but I had the Kongo staff in my hand." (p. 181), however he does not mention a hat or bag. At first, the only actual proof of what he used during the pilgrimage is a copy of an *osamefuda* (name-slip) with his name and address, which is located in the Appendix of his book (see 85C, enlarged copy: Picture 1). I asked Hanna about the existence of other items of pilgrim attire that he might have used and that might still be in their possession. She stated that she was certain that the hat had been thrown away, but thought someone in the family might have his vest, staff and bag. She asked her siblings to look around, and as a result, they discovered his *osamefuda* (name-slip) box with his name on the back, some blank *osamefuda* (Picture 2), and his long white pilgrim coat with the red stamps from each temple (Picture 3,4).

Picture 1

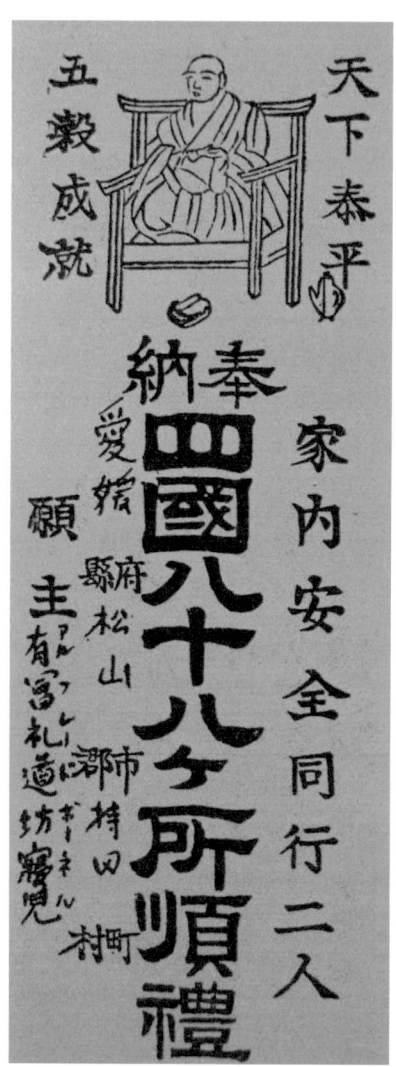

Picture 2

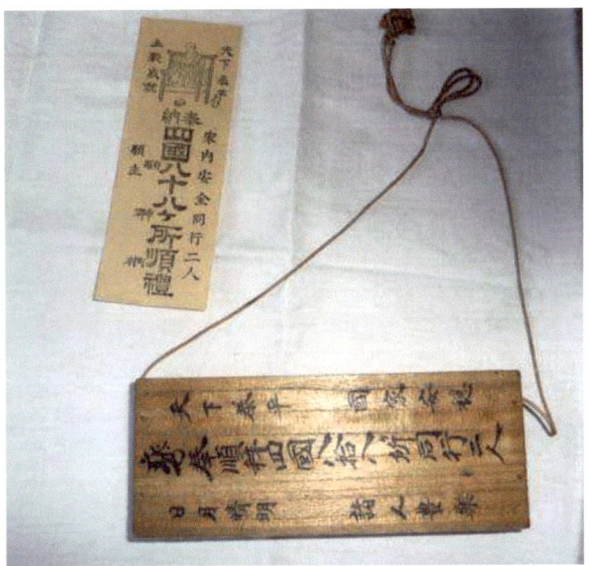

Osamefuda and osamefuda box

Picture 3

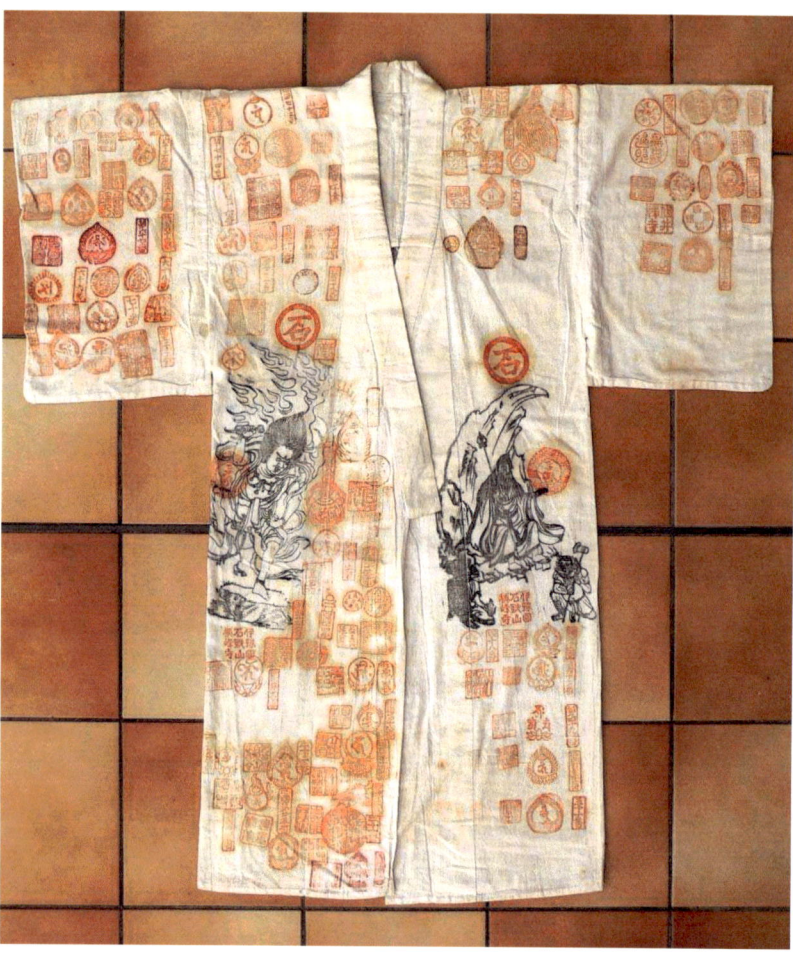

Pilgrim coat (front)

Picture 4

Pilgrim coat (back)

Editor's note: About this English edition

The University of Hawaii at Manoa provided a scanned PDF file of the English manuscript; however, the quality was not good so I retyped the entire content for this publication. Any possible mistakes or missing words due to this transcription are my own fault.

Alfred Bohner mistakenly read some of the characters in book titles and temple names, etc., and Katharine Merrill did not change them. In such cases, I have left them in the original form; however, the correct readings are as follows:

For example:

1. The book title, *Shikoku-do Shi-nan*, should be *Shikoku Michishirube*.

2. *Dōgyō Futari* should be *Dōgyō Ninin*

3. *Henrei* should be *Henro*

4. The name of temple No. 1 is not Reisan-ji, but Ryozen-ji. As well, I have not attempted to correct any possible factual errors.

In some places I have added a footnote (i.e. Editor -) with supplementary information and have attempted to smooth out portions of the manuscript that do not read smoothly.

Alfred Bohner writes Japanese names with the surname last, so I have not changed this format.

A Supplement to the Proceedings of the German Society
for the Study of the Countries and Peoples of East Asia.

Supplement XII

Two on a Pilgrimage
The 88 Holy Places of Shikoku

By Alfred Bohner
(English translation by Katharine Merrill)

With 88 illustrations and 1 map

Tokyo
1931

The German Society for the Study of
The Countries and Peoples of East Asia

18 Hirakawa-cho, 5-chome, Kojimachi-ku

Illustration from the book *Shikoku-do Shi-nan*:
Two pilgrims (man and woman) and a porter

Preface

The first incentive to write this book was a lecture that I was privileged to give in Tokyo last autumn before the Society for the Study of the Countries and Peoples of East Asia. When I accepted the kind invitation of the committee I set to prepare the lecture materials for publication. As a result, I gradually acquired such an abundance of material that I had difficulty in arranging it all, especially since I was greatly restricted by a desire not to let the book become too rich in detail. Therefore, the readers, especially those acquainted with Shikoku, may feel that there is a lot missing, since there was room for scarcely a third of the available photographs. This lack of space was also a restriction, so I gave up including a minute description of each temple and of its history, and had to be satisfied with giving in addition to a general account of the pilgrim journey and the founding of the temples only a list in the Appendix of the 88 holy places of pilgrimage. For the same reason, the collection of sayings and legends about Kōbō Daishi current in Shikoku, as well as the description of several festivals, such as *goma-shugyō, kaichō,* and *fuda-nagashi*, originally prepared for the Appendix, had to be omitted.

I regret every much that I lack a general education in theology, as well as a knowledge of Shingon, adequate for doing justice to such religious questions as cannot be avoided in the book, and I find these deficiencies all the more grievous when, under the influence of Witte's *Japan Between Two Cultures*[14], I am brought to a new realization of how important the comprehension of religious Japan is for a general understanding of the country. It was therefore necessary to resign myself again and again to basing my opinion on living personal impressions, and to forego the satisfaction of having scientific proof for my statements.

I am, therefore, all the more grateful for the support which has come to my work from the most diversified sources. My colleagues at the Matsuyama Koto Gakko – Professors Eiichirō Suzuki, Shinya Uchida, Bunjō Ōe, Ai Shigematsu (now at Fukuoka University), Junjirō Ide and Jun-ichirō Kitagawa – never wearied of answering his numberless questions, while Professor Chokkō Kageura and Messrs. Gentō Saionji, Tan Soga and Kikutarō Kan

of the Historical Society of Iyo (Iyo Shidankai) placed their valuable material at my disposal in the most kind and helpful way. Furthermore, Mr. Shigehiro Ishioka of Daion-ji in Tachibana showed himself to be a true supporter through all the phases of the task, from the procur-

---

[14] Editor: The book is *Japan zwischen zwei Kulturen* by Johannes Witte, 1928. Published by J.C. Hinrichs, Leipzig, Germany.

ing of the pilgrim dress and outfit to the end of the manuscript. Some priests of the 88 temples also assisted me in
carrying out his project, not the least among these being
the help received from Mr. Ryūdō Tanshoyo, the abbot of
Hantaji (No.50) near Matsuyama. Sincere thanks are here
given to them all, and together with them Dr. Wilhelm
Gundert[15] and Mr. Kurt Meissner[16] of Tokyo for the kindly
interest that they have taken in this work, the latter for a
gift of a photograph as well.

A year ago today I returned from the pilgrimage.
Personal considerations forced me in March of this year to
return to Germany and to say farewell to the Island-of-the-Four-Provinces, which had become dear to me.
I beg leave, however, to let this book serve as a promise
that in my homeland also I will continue to work for better
understanding between East and West, and as the expression of my hope of returning again in years to come to my
old field of work.

Mittelberg in Walsertel, August 5, 1928
(Vorarlberg)
Alfred Bohner

---

[15] Editor – Gundert (1880-1971)
[16] Editor – During World War I, Meissner was in the German
army stationed at Tsingtao. He was captured by the Japanese
forces and spent time as a PoW in the Bando camp in Tokushima.
He once wrote an article about the Shikoku pilgrimage for the
camp newsletter and remained in Japan after the war.

Translator's Note

For three years, from 1924 to 1927, I was privileged to know the author, Alfred Bohner, and his family in Matsuyama. We share an interest in and a love for Japan and her people. When, over ten years ago, Alfred sent the book to me, with permission to translate it into English, it was with delight that I set to work on this project. But due to the pressure of regular duties, it has been impossible to finish the work earlier.

I feel unfit for the task, but as I also feel that such an interesting and significant book should be available to English readers and students of Japanese customs, so I have ventured to undertake the translation. I wish to acknowledge a great deal of help from Professor Josef Koerber (of the Matsuyama Koto Gakko, 1929 to 1935) and from Prau Barbara Boener, wife of the present German professor in Matsuyama, both of whom have given of their time in helping to solve knotty bits of translation. As well to. Mr. Frank Cary, formerly of Matsuyama, whose library furnished the original wording of the English quotations from Lloyd and Reischauer, I am also indebted.

The task has been undertaken in a spirit of recreation rather than of work, and I hope that others will enjoy and profit by reading the book, and will thereby wide and deepen their knowledge of Japan as much as I have done.

Katharine Merrill

Matsuyama Shinonome Kōtō Jo Gakkō[17]

Matsuyama, Japan, 1941.

---

[17] Editor – Matsuyama Shinonome Girl's High School.

Table of Contents

Introduction: The Shikoku pilgrimage:
A National Phenomenon of Japan

For centuries there have been numerous Buddhist pilgrimages in Japan. The custom of making a pilgrimage originated in India, the home of Buddhism, where soon after Gautama's death people began to make pilgrimages to eight, later to ten, temples that were especially significant either because of Gautama's relation to them or because of the possession of his ashes. This custom was carried on from very early times and moved from India to China, where it was given the name *ehinhsiang* (in Japanese: *shinkō*, an offering of incense). Upon the introduction of Buddhism to Japan, this religious rite began in Japan. Even if the year or the decade cannot be exactly determined, there is no doubt that the most ancient pilgrimage in Japan, is that to the Seven Great Temples of the Southern Capital (*Nanto Shichidai-ji*) which was already in existence from around the middle of the Heian period (c. 1000AD). As well, at that time the inhabitants of Kyoto who could not make this pilgrimage were accustomed to go instead to the seven Kannon temples of Rokujizō (*Rokujizō Shichik-wannon*) between the cities of Kyoto and Otsu.

Among the pilgrimages, which even today have special importance, the most significant ones are to the 33 temples of Bandō (*Bandō Sanjūsannkasho*), to the 34 temples of Chichibu (*Chichibu Sanjūyonkasho*), to the 33 Kwannon temples of Saikoku (*Saikoku sanjūsankasho*), and to the 88 Holy places of Shikoku (*Shikoku Hachijūhakkasho*). However, no pilgrimage among those listed or among any of the pilgrimages not mentioned has more significance for the life of the people of Japan, or has become to a greater extent ingrained in the life of the nation than the pilgrimage in Shikoku. Although this pilgrimage is known far and wide in the land, and had already been imitated to some degree during the Kan-ei era (1624-1643) by 88 temples in Tokyo and its environs --- such an imitation can be seen today in numerous provinces --- there was for a long time no one who could give me an explanation of the pilgrimage of Bandō until at Rinnō-ji temple in Nikko when I found a inscription that declared it to be the 17th of the Bando temples. I was happy to have come at last into possession of the desired information. I then went to the place where the copyists were sitting, but none of the four acolytes who were present could tell me where the rest of the temples were; even the location and the name of the next temple were unknown to them. The only thing that I could get out of them was the fact that the first temples were situated in Tokyo, and that the temple of Kwannon in Asakusa was the third in the series.

The Saikoku pilgrimage is much more important than other pilgrimages. It takes precedence over the Shikoku pilgrimage in age, even although up to the present it has not been possible to prove the tradition of its establishment by the Emperor Kwasan (c. 984AD). This pilgrimage begins at Nachiyama in the province of Kii, goes through Izumi, Kawachi, Yamato (Nara), Yamashiro, Omi, Kyoto, Tanba, Settsu, Harima, Tango, back to Omi, and ends in the province of Mino at Tanigumiyama. The very number of the provinces included in the pilgrimage shows what a large territory it covers. There the temples lie so far apart, the connection between them is naturally somewhat less close, and the character of the pilgrimage is lost to a certain degree. Even if the pilgrims were as numerous as they are on the Shikoku pilgrimage, they would vanish in the midst of other traffic on a journey that is many times the length of the one on Shikoku, and which leads as well through some of the most thickly settled parts of Japan, and they would leave scarcely any impressions upon the life of the people such as pilgrims do on the Island-of-the-Four-Provinces. Besides, since the Saikoku pilgrimage, wholly aside from the actual performance of it, places incomparably greater financial burdens on the pilgrims, it is undertaken as a whole by a relatively small number of believers. Most people content themselves with completing it upon one of the substitute ways which are scattered over the land, as are those of the 88 places of Shikoku. The significance of the 33 Kwannon temples, therefore, lies much more in the realm of history: these temples appear in novels and in dreams of the Tokugawa period as a background for the action; Buddhist legends and religious poetry owe much inspiration to them; and in the art of religious singing or chanting, the songs of the Kwannon Temples, called *go-eika*, which because of their lofty poetical value stand out conspicuously among all other products of Japanese devotional literature, have even today great influence upon other parts of Japan. Even so, it is not improbable that other pilgrimages, not excepting that of Shikoku, are modeled upon the 33 temples of Kwannon. In regard to its significance for the life of the people of today, however, the pilgrimage of Saikoku, to say nothing of the others, cannot be compared to that of Shikoku. Even though isolated temples here and there attract great numbers of believers, the pilgrims nowhere else stream in greater numbers through the countryside, and nowhere else does the population take a greater interest in them than in the Island-of-the-Four-Provinces. The pilgrim must travel over 1200 kilometers; he must give up his usual manner of life and his daily work for weeks, in some cases for months; he must entrust his household, his store, and his workshop to other; by day he must climb high mountains by difficult paths, and he must descend into the valley by ways just as uncomfortable, or even by the rough bed of a half-dried-up mountain stream, in order to arrive in the evening at miserable lodgings, with a wretched bed and slender fare, until at the end he may lay down his heavy burden for the last time, put aside his pilgrim's staff, and take off his pilgrim's garb. Every year tens of thousands of Japanese take this pilgrimage and have undertaken it for hundreds of years.[18] But every year charitable people along the pilgrim roads give food, drink and other gifts to the pilgrims in such a degree that is not dreamed of in modern cities, even in those in Japan. And this custom has been going on for centuries! A guidebook from 1689 highlights certain places where gifts flow more profusely, and in one place even alludes by name to a man who for seven years has furnished every pilgrim with a pair of straw sandals. A philological inquiry into the expressions and phrases in the language of the people of Shikoku which have some connection with the pilgrimage or with its spiritual originator, Kōbō Daishi, would certainly give much information about the close connection between the pilgrimage and the life of the people in gen-

---

[18] The estimates vary. I have heard 30,000 to 40,000 quoted as the number of those who complete the pilgrimage in a year; on the contrary, according to the Shorō Teraishi (see Bibliography), the priest of the 38th temple in Tosa estimates the number as substantially lower, when he says that it never falls below 20,000. The assertion of Chamberlain in *Things Japanese* (p. 371) that the custom of going on pilgrimage is decreasing does not in the least accord with my experience and with statements in regard to the Shikoku pilgrimage.

eral. To be sure, through such a study the pilgrim, or at least one class of them to be described in detail later, would often show up in a bad light, since for example we discover that *shugyō* (religious practice) is a word also used in Shikoku as a synonym for begging.[19]

---

[19] A list, by no means complete, of expressions and phrases from the language of the pilgrims is to be found in the Appendix.

Main Section:
The 88 Holy Places of Shikoku

A: History of the pilgrimage

I: Kōbō Daishi – the spiritual founder

Concerning the origin and the exact date of the beginning of the pilgrimage to the 88 temples, the sources leave us much in the dark as in the case of the other pilgrimages. Nevertheless, tradition traces the establishment of the 88 places back to Kōbō Daishi, the founder of the Shingon sect in Japan. Even though, as we shall see later, there are presently grave doubts regarding this belief, yet his personality dominates the pilgrimage to such a degree that we can with assurance, nay, we even must, declare him as the spiritual founder. For the pilgrim does not take his journey alone, he takes it together with Kōbō Daishi. *Shikoku Hachijūhakkasho Reijō Henrei Dōgyō Futari* (A Pilgrimage of Two to the 88 Holy Places of Shikoku), is the real name of the pilgrimage. Our companion is Kōbō Daishi; he goes with us in the form of our pilgrim staff; we must even take with us provisions and footgear for him. Our first task, therefore, is to become better acquainted with him. Fortunately, there are a great number of biographies from a comparatively early period. These are, to be sure, almost without exception in the Chinese style, of which the oldest, written in the year of Kūkai's death by his favorite pupil, Shinzei, has appeared lately in a Japanese translation. The only biography older than this is written in the Japanese style is to be found in twelve illustrated rolls, which are preserved in the To-ji temple in Kyoto, and which go back several centuries, since they were inspected by the Emperor Go Kōmyo (1338-1350). This biography was printed in the collection of Kokubun Tōhō Bukkyō Gyōsho after it had already appeared once in the Tempo Era (1833) as a woodcut book. (For the remaining biographies, in so far as they were used for this work, see Bibliographical References, at the end of the book.)

A critical compilation of the collected source material on Kōbō Daishi's life and works can be found in the very exhaustive book, *Kōbō Daishi Den no Kenkyū*, by Shinnosuke Makino (Kyoto, 1921), which gives in a bibliographical appendix of 37 items an estimation of all the more important works. The merit of having translated into German one of the countless biographies that were written in an edifying fashion belongs to Superintendent Dr. Schiller of Kyoto, while as early as the year 1905 there appeared in the newspaper "Wahrheit" (Truth) a short essay in German from the pen of Professor H. Minami.

Kōbō Daishi, "Master of the Propagation of the Doctrine", is really a posthumous name of honour (*chokushi*) that was bestowed upon the master eighty-six years after his death in the year 921 by the Emperor Daigo, Through comparison and supplementing of the "*Annalen des japanischen Buddhismus"* (Annals of Japanese Buddhism) by Haas[20], I was able to determine the following twenty official bearers of the title of Daishi, that is, those so designated by a Japanese emperor:

Priests' name	Year of Death	Daishi Name	Year of Bestowal
Saichō	822	Dengyō Daishi	866
Kūkai	835	Kōbō Daishi	921
Jitsue	845	Dōkō Daishi	1774
Ennin	864	Jikaku Daishi	866
Shinga	879	Hōkō Daishi	1828
Yakushin	906	Hongaku Daishi	1308
Shōbō	909	Rigen Daishi	1707
Ryōgen	985	Jie Daishi	987
Ryōnin	1138	Shōō Daishi	1773
Kakuban	1149	Kōgyō Daishi	1690[21]
Dōgen	1200	Shōyō Daishi	1880
Genkū (Hōnen)	1212	Enkō Daishi	1697
Shunshō	1227	Getsurin Daishi	1883
Shinren	1262	Kenshin Daishi	1876
Chichin (Ippen Shōnin)	1289	Enshō Daishi	1886
Shinshō[22]	1495	Jisshō Daishi	1883

[20] Editor – The book is by Hans Haas, 1908, published by Druck der Nobunsho, Tokyo.
[21] The number of the year which I found in the *Bukkyō Daijiten* and in other places does not always agree with that given by Haas (1692).

Kenju (Rennyo Shōnin)	1499	Etō Daishi	1882
Tenkai	1643	Jigen Daishi	1651

As one can see from this list, some received the title within the first ten years after their death, and therefore before a long enough interval of time had elapsed to judge of their lasting worth. On the other hand, the warlike Nichiren had to wait until quite recently for official recognition. Quite apart from the undisputed worthiness of such distinguished men, there was also in the honors which were bestowed upon them in the 1870s and 1880s a strong desire to offer reconciliation again to the Buddhists who had suffered all sorts of persecution after the Restoration. There is an exception in the case of Hōnen Shōnin (1133-1212)[23], to whom not less than five emperors gave the title of Daishi (1697, 1711, 1761, 1811, 1861). The first title given him is the best known.[24]

---

[22] The "Bulletin de la Maison Franco-Japonaise" writes mistakenly "Shinzei" and "Jitsshō Daishi", as well as "Shōhō" instead of the usual "Shōbō."

[23] Editor – He was a monk of the Tendai sect, but later founded the Jodo sect (The Pure Land School).

[24] Strangely enough, the "Bulletin de la Maison Franco-Japonaise" writes Enkō Meishō (instead of Myōhō) Daishi, which agrees neither with the statements of the Bukkyō Daijiten nor with those of the Bukkyō Jimmei Jiten, and is also contrary to the custom of writing the name of the Daishi with only two characters. The title Daisi came from China, where likewise it was bestowed upon famous priests, as for example,

Kūkai is therefore not the first in the course of history to have received a title of reverence, but as the proverb says, "*Taiko wa Hideyoshi ni torare, Daishi wa Kōbō ni torareru.*" (Hideyoshi has taken the title of Taiko, Kōbō that of Daishi, unto himself), so it is in reality, and not only in Shikoku. If the Daishi is spoken of, Kōbō Daishi is meant. The given name of this priest is seldom heard, and his family name never. His family name was really Saeki. He was born in the year 774[25] according to our reckoning, the son of the ruler of the province of Sanuki, Count Saeki no Atai Yoshimichi, in Byōbu-ga-Ura, in the district of Tado. For a long time the location of his birthplace was a matter of dispute, and in the Bunkwa Era (1804-1818) there was even a downright quarrel between the Kaigan-ji at Tadotsu

---

upon the first patriarch of the Tendai sect, Chiki, called Chisha Daishi (both Japanese pronunciations). Japanese priests also of the Tendai and the Rinzai sects have received the title from China. Finally, there are yet others such as Gishin (d826) who were called Daishi by the common people without ever having received the title officially (Gishin=Shuzen Daishi; Enchō=Jakkō Daishi, Chiki=Tenda Daishi). Another title which was earlier bestowed by the Emperor is Kokushi (a teacher of the country); for example, one who received it was Kakushin (d1293), the founder of komusō, those flute-playing priests whom one still sees everywhere today travelling around the country with their faces wholly concealed by huge bell-shaped hats. He is called Hōtō Kokushi.

[25] The date given by Lloyd in "The Development of Japanese Buddhism" is false. (Translator's note: Later in "The Greed of Half Japan" (1911) Lloyd gives the correct date, 774)

and the Zentsū-ji, a dispute which was settled at that time by the Solomon-like decision that Kōbō was born, to be sure, in Zentsū-ji, but received his first education in Kaigan-ji. The uncertainty, however, still persisted, until a few years ago Professor Chokkō Kageura proved through minute and disinterested comparisons of place names that the honor of the birthplace should fall to Zentsū-ji, a decision which was followed some months later, almost as if in confirmation, by the discovery, in the course of some construction work by the 11th Division stationed there, or two seals with the name of Kūkai. Kūkai (Ethereal Sea, Heavenly Sea) is the name which Kōbō Daishi bore for the longest time in his life. The names that he gave to himself in the course of his life or that were given to him are:

Maō -"True Fish"- The first name he was known as a child
Tōtomo-"Worthy of Veneration" - Given by his parents to their precious child as a sign of love and veneration
Shindō - "Child of God" - What the neighbors called the eight or nine-year-old boy
Kyōkai - "See of Learning" - The name given him when he left his father's house
Nyokū - "Like the Ether" - His second name as a priest
Mukū - "Empty and void" - His third name as a priest
Kūkai - "Ethereal Sea" or "Sea of Emptiness" - The name adopted when he received holy orders (gusoKūkai), ap-

parently made up of earlier names put together.

Gohitsu Wajō - "Abbot of the Five Writing Brushes" - A name given to him by the Chinese Emperor as a sign of distinction because of his art with the brush as shown in the palace.

Henjō Kongō - "Diamond Illuminating All" - A name bestowed upon him when he was consecrated the Patriarch of the Shingon Sect.

As we have seen above, Kūkai came of a very good family. His father was a descendant in the eighth generation of the Emperor Keikō; on his mother's side we find in the family of Atō some of the best known scholars and artists of their time. We may therefore assume that his spiritual and religious talent came chiefly from his mother's side, whereas from his father came those eminently practical aspects of his character that were to show themselves in the most diverse ways. It was an uncle on his mother's side, Atō Sukune no Ōtani, tutor in the household of Prince Iyo, who first discovered in the boy his uncommon talents, who instructed him in the Analects of Confucius and other Chinese writings, and also persuaded his parents to let him[26] go to Kyoto in the year 788 where three years later he entered the university. Famous teachers like

---

[26] The pilgrim biographies say here, "the only child", in order to make the sacrifice appear still greater, but that is not historic.

Umazake no Kiyonari, know far and wide at that time as a universal historian, and Okaa no Hakase, soon exhausted their knowledge on him. With them he studied chiefly Confucianism and Taoism, but he was not satisfied, and in 793[27] he accepted the invitation of Gonzō, the virtuous abbot of Makiozan Temple in Izumi, from whom he learned the memory-strengthening teaching, the so-called *Gumonji*. Soon Buddhism had taken the young man prisoner, he decided henceforth to devote his life to it, and took the first vows. But although he was committed to belief, he still had all kinds of doubts, and he wanted absolute certainty. He therefore prayed continually for a teaching which, contrary to that with which he was already acquainted, would bring him peace, and he is said finally to have had a dream in which the way was shown him to a temple, Kumedera in Yamato Province, where he should find a certain sutra that could put an end to his doubts. He found there the Dainichikyō[28], upon which the Shingon sect is based, but now it appeared that there were several places in it that no one in Japan could explain to him, and he definitely made up his mind to go to China.[29]

---

[27] Makino wrongly places this in his chronological table in the year 798, contrary to most of the biographics and to the will (ikoku) of Kūkai.

[28] Mahavairokana-sutra, No. 530, by Nanjō.

[29] Exact information about Kūkai's life and activities for the years, 799-803 (first half) and still later for the year 820 are lacking; in

He finally succeeded in obtaining the necessary permission from the Emperor; in June 804, he departed from the coast of Kyushu in the retinue of the Imperial Messenger, Fujiwara Ason Kadano Maro, and after thirty-four days reached China in August. There from the beginning he distinguished himself by his knowledge of Chinese. The ship had been driven by storms farther south than Japanese ships had been used to travelling, and had put into the land of Foochow in the province of Fukion.[30] Here the people did not want to let the delegation land, since they did not understand the explanations of the messengers. Not until Kūkai set forth the circumstances of the journey in a document written in Chinese and still preserved in the original wording, were the messenger and his retinue allowed to land, and in December of the same year they reach the capital Chang-an, the Shi-an of today. Kūkai lost no time, but immediately got into touch with famous priests and received instructions from them.

Of the greatest significance form his meeting with

---

general, it is assumed that the period of his seclusion on Cape Muroto, of which he speaks in his will, fell in the period between 799-803.

[30] Of four ships that set out at the same time only the one in which Saichō (Dengyō Daishi), the founder of the Tendai sect in Japan, travelled, reached its destination, the port called today Ningpo in the province of Chakisag. Two ships could not continue on the journey, and one disappeared.

Huikuo (Keika or Eka[31], in Japanese), the abbot of the Tsinglung Temple (Seiryū-ji[32], in Japanese), and seven patriarchs of the Shingon sect. As Simeon once greeted the tiny child Jesus, so the hoary patriarch greeted the young Japanese priest. He walked towards him, and with a smile lighting his old features said, "I have been waiting long for thee. My sojourn upon this earth has already been too long. Prepare thyself therefore to receive the teaching."[33]

---

[31] Among the three readings which Haas uses confusedly side by side without saying that they concern the same person, the "Bulletin de la Maison France-Japonaise" gives preference to the reading Eka, but in the Shingon sect it is always read Keika. (Editor – Hui-kuo (746-805)).

[32] Mistakenly read Serin-ji by Lloyd.

[33] This greeting is rather well accredited. Moreover, it does not exclude but on the contrary says much for the fact that Kūkai learned about Christianity also in Chang-an. Under the Chinese Emperor Tai-Tsung in the year 635 missionaries of the Nestorian Church had come there and had begun their missionary work. The emperor, originally addicted to Confucianism and rather averse to Buddhism and Taoism make their work easy in every respect, so that at the time that Kūkai came to Chang-an there were already four large flourishing churches there. Moreover, the holy scriptures of the Nestorians had been translated into Chinese and were incorporated in the great library, which Tai-tsung and his successor, Changsun, erected. It is improbable that Kūkai, who pursued his studies in every imaginable direction, should have passed by those places of Nestorian worship, arresting to the eye by their manner of building, without informing this, he must surely have seen, as Mrs. E.A. Gordon, from whose little book, *Kōbō Daishi to Keikyō* (Kōbō Daishi and Nestorian Christianity), we take these statements, rightly asserts, the great monument, three meters high and

Huikuo himself baptized Kūkai in the new doctrine. Blindfolded Kūkai stepped upon the platform, holding between his hands the branch of the star anise. Twice he had to let it fall, so that the godhead under whose protection he was to stand henceforth might declare himself, once for the Kongōkai, the world of eternally unshakable ideas, and again for the Taizōkai, the world of phenomena. Both times the branch fell upon the portrait of Dainichi Nyorai. Kūkai was therefore regarded as the incarnation of Dainichi Nyorai, and since his name in the Kongōkai in Kongō (Diamond), but in the Taizōkai in Henjō (Giving light to all), Kūkai received the two names, "Henjō Kongō" (That which gives light to all, the Diamond."

Abbot Huikuo now had some of his students paint the pictures of the Paradise (Mandara) of the Kongōkai and of the Taizōkai that were contained in the secret books of Shingon, as well as the portraits of the earlier patriarchs, eleven patriarchs in all. Over twenty writers of sutras had to copy to sutras and in the shastras, more than 100 in all,

---

one-and-a-half meters wide, that was erected in Chang-an in the year 781, twenty-three years before Kūkai's arrival, and that set forth briefly in 1700 characters the teaching of the Nestorians and the spread of the doctrine in China. (A facsimile of the statue is to the seen at Koya-san, presented by Mrs. Gordon). On the other hand, there is not a single reference to Christianity or to Mohammedanism in the book of the ten stages of the heart, in which Kūkai depicts ten stages of belief, arranging in order in it the other religions and sects.

while the workers in bronze had to prepare a new set of the implements of the cult, fifteen in number, bells, *sankō* (tridents; vajr in Sanskrit), *gokō* (five-pronged implements), *rin* (wheels), and columns of brass for the baptismal font. In addition, Huikuo committed to Kūkai's care even more valuable relics of all sorts, and by the time of his death in December of the following year had entrusted to him his whole teaching. Daishi wrote the lament for the dead and the epitaph, which have come down to us. Then he continued his studies in Sanskrit and in the art of writing in another temple, and even had the honor of being invited by the Emperor Hsientsung to exhibit proofs of his art on the walls of the Imperial Palace, a task that brought him the name of "Master of the Five Writing Brushes." Through his poems and his literary style also he is said to have won universal admiration.

Now however the urge came upon him to return as quickly as he could to Japan and to spread abroad the new teaching. He obtained permission to leave from the Emperor, who on his occasion made him another special gift; nobles and scholars accompanied him to the ship; and in August 806, he left China, to land safely after two months in Kyushu, where his first task was to draw up a careful inventory of all the treasures which he had brought with him, and to send it, together with the announcement of his return, to the court in the capital. He was invited to come to Kyoto. (one line illegible) From this name arose later the legend that he has written with five brushes at the same time. The years that followed we find him now in the palace, where in addition to his religious activity he instructed the Emperor in the arts of writing and of poetry, and now travelling around the country in places as far away as Nikko. Priesthood in various temples was conferred upon him, as for example, in Todai-ji in Nara, where in the year 813 he founded the temple Nan-endo. In the year 810 in a hall of the palace he took part in a discussion with the chief priests of other sects in order to clear himself of the charges of heterodoxy and of heresy, and especially to prove from the sutras the authority of the secret teachings of Shingon. Although he fought his way through to a complete victory, he felt that the capital and the court were not the right place for his teaching to flourish. Much as he appeared on the one hand to be a sophisticated courtier, on the other hand his secret teaching drew his just as powerfully into the loneliness of a remote, inaccessible mountain peak. As he had once fled when a young man of twenty-five or twenty-six from the confusion of the capital into the wilderness of Cape Muroto, "Where" in the words of one of his poems, "year in, year out, nor wind nor waves subside," so again in the year 816 he requested a place in the mountains of the Kii peninsula where the tradition of his teaching could be maintained. His request was granted; he ascended Mount Koya (816) to lay the foundation of the *kondō*, which was destroyed by fire in the year 1926. At that time he is said to have written the poem, *"Iro ha ni ho he to,"* in order to encourage the carpenters in their work; or, according to another version (mentioned by Ronshō Kwanzan, p53), in order to indicate the grooves and pegs of the beams belonging together, and so at the same to have established the order of the Japanese syllabary.[34]

After the founding of the Kondō and of the depository of the sutras (*Kyōzō*), he went again on a journey through the eastern part of Japan, but in the year 821 we find him in his home province of Sanuki, the ruler of which had invited him to plan artificial pools for the irrigation of the rice fields. This is the only time in Kūkai's biography that a visit to Shikoku in his later years is expressly mentioned. If he really was the first to undertake the pilgrimage around the island, such a journey must have taken place, if not in his youth, in this year. In the following year he was already back in Nara, where the Emperor Heijō,

---

[34] Recent research considers if rather impossible that Kūkai was the author of the poem, even if it is admitted that the author is to be sought in priestly circles. The chief argument is that the metric form 7-5-7-5 belongs to the end of the Heian period (794-1192). On the other hand, Kūkai, as Lange (Hinfuhrung in die japanische Schrift, p3) has already remarked, cannot be considered the origantor of kana, since the use of these signs before his time has been proved. Those who nevertheless consider him the author of the poem see therein an anticipation of the later meter, and therefore a new proof of Kūkai's genius.

who had abdicated, received baptism from him in Tōdai-ji. In the next year the ruling Emperor Saga abdicated, after he had previously given Kūkai the Tō-ji temple in Kyoto as a base for the spread of the teaching of the Shingon sect.[35] Emperor Saga also let himself be baptized by Kūkai.

During the last decade of his life Kūkai did something that was significant in his character as master. He like no one else understood how to find the corresponding education between the Shinto and the Buddhist pantheons. Here, the highest Shinto divinity, Amaterasu O Mikami, is identified with the central figure of the Shingon pantheon, Dainichi Nyorai and in order to promote this education he founded in Kyoto the Shūgei Shuchiin[36], an institution that might perhaps be designated as the first forerunner of the institutes for comparing the science of religion, and where Buddhism, Confucianism, Taoism, etc., were taught side by side. Two years later he even wrote a ten-volume work in which he discussed and criticized the various beliefs, and explained the secret teachings of Shingon. Since Kungtse and Laotse are designated by him as incarnations of Judo Bosatsu and Kashō Bosatsu, the introduction of Confucianism and also of Taoism into his building of the

---

[35] The chief temple of the sect enforced the closing of all branches of Shingon during the Meiji era. The various branches have, however, kept naturally to their particular chief temples.
[36] The reading Sōgei Shuchiin (Reischauer, and others) is incorrect.

Shingon teaching is made much easier.

The last years of his life Kūkai were divided among Koya-san, Takao-san in Kyoto prefecture and To-ji in Kyoto city. When, however, he felt his end drawing near, he had himself carried to Koya, where he died on the 3rd of March, 835, and where he is buried. The chapel above his grave forms today the most holy place (*okunoin*) of the whole temple mountain.

I have omitted from this short biographical sketch as much as possible of the material which, upon comparison with the various descriptions of his life that have been handed down, proved to be more legendary ornament. The books intended especially for the simple, common people cannot treat enough of the marvelous, while the oldest sources are more reserved, and in recent works, as for example in "Kaizō izen in okeru Koya-san Bunkashi" by Hōjō Nakata, a young historian of Koya-san, and by Makino (in a book mentioned above), there is doubt expressed, although cautiously, even of the history of the founding of this mountain institution.

If one includes the countless legends, the many parallels to the life of Christ are remarkable. We find the story of the Annunciation in the form of a vision in a dream; a wonderful birth (a strange radiance lights up the room); like Jesus in the Apocryphal stories about Him, the young Daishi also shows himself different from other chil-

children, as he forms images of Buddha out of clay and adores them, builds pagodas and temples out of twigs and stalks and places his images in them, and so forth; the adoration of the three Kings finds its counterpart in two stories, the one of a famous priest who recognized the crying of the child as sounds from Sanskrit and prophesied a great future for him, and the other of an Imperial Messenger who visited the district and knelt down before the playing Daishi; like Jesus, he too as a twelve-year-old boy was already mature in wisdom and understanding; he too left his parents behind for higher calling; like the Nazarene, he withdrew to the solitude of Cape Muroto, where he was tempted by devils[37]; like Jesus upon the Lake of Gennesaret, he too upon the return voyage from China calmed the wind and the waves that threatened to sink the ship; again and again he left the capital and the court, where

---

[37] Schiller puts the story of the temptation over against the legend according to which the six- (by Japanese court, seven) year-old boy hurls himself from a rock in order to obtain assurance as to whether he is called to save other people. Shaka appears in a cloud and leads him back to where he had been standing. Aside from the fact that not even in the Bible is there lacking the conception underlying this legend, that is, that man is authorized in certain critical hours to demand a sign that God is with him and his task, this episode at Cape Muroto appears tous to offer many more likenesses, since temptation by the powers of darkness of a person withdrawn into solitude is the subject in both cases.

honours and dignities were heaped upon him and where the friendship of the Emperor tried to detain him, and travelled throughout the country, instructing and teaching the people; and when the pilgrim today prays his "*Namu Daishi Henjō Kongō*" (I believe in the Master who brings light to all, the Diamond), and believes in the concept of *sokushin jōbutsu*, the attainment of Buddhahood in this body, he thinks no further of the complicated teaching of Shingon: the Daishi and his grace (*go riyaku*) take the same place with him as Jesus Christ and his words do with a believing Christian: "Whoso believeth in me shall live, even though he die."

But to the prayers that the pilgrim prays before each temple belong also the Shingon and Dharani invocations of the Buddhist divinations, those remarkable Japanese transcriptions of old Sanskrit words, and when the pilgrim stays overnight in a temple, he often takes part in the goma-festival, which we can translate only unsatisfactorily by "fire mass", and which is one of the first, and, so it is said, one of the most effective practices of the secret teaching of Shingon. And in that we see Kūkai from another side: we see him as the founder of the Japanese *mikkyō* (secret teaching).[38] It is remarkable that the same

[38] Schiller writes falsely mikyō, Reischauer also falsely himitsu-kyō. A brief statement of the teaching of the Shingon sect is to be found in Lloyd's "Development of Japanese Buddhism" (pp392,ff). The way to magic is briefly summarized in the fol-

man who was possessed as few people are of a clear spirit and a practical mind; who busied himself in China not only with Sanskrit and Chinese, but also with the learning of all possible arts and skills – with the production of India ink and the making of writing brushes, with the preparation of cakes as well as with the building of houses --; he who understood as few people did how to share with others the knowledge he had gained; who showed the charcoal burners in Tosa how to make air-holes in their charcoal kilns[39]; who showed the inhabitants of Echigo the various possibilities in the use of petroleum[40]: it is remarkable, I repeat, that it should have been this very man who founded one of the most abstruse secret teachings in

---

lowing train of thought: The realm of ideas is the source of all things. If I have the right ideas I can rule matter. But I express ideas through words. So the 'true word' (Shingon) becomes a magic word, the effective cause of the wished for appearances. Therefore, he who knows the magic words can attain to what he will when he simply thinks or expresses such thoughts in words. The in, that is, seals, certain methods of folding the hands have a meaning similar to these various words.

[39] In South Tosa, as a head woodman told me, the holes in charcoal-kilns are to this day called *O Daishi no ana* (holes of the Daishi). The importation of barley into Tosa brings one temple (No.34) into connection with Kōbō Daishi; in another place he is name as the introducer of mortar, while the legend of the Yanagi-mizu (between the 11th and 12th temples) is pointed out as a use of the conjuring-stick.

[40] The presence of petroleum in Echigo was historically proved as early as 668AD, since in that year the people of Echigo offered as a gift to the Emperor Tenchi moyuru mizu (burnable water).

Japan, with its complicated symbolism of words, its form of magic, and its exorcisms.

It is, therefore, not to be wondered at that, together with recognition of his extraordinary accomplishments on the professional side, very severe judgment has been passed on Kōbō Daishi. Kūkai can lay claim to no originality, says Schiller; in that respect he is a typical Japanese, in that he has understood exceedingly well how to pass on to his own countrymen ideas and things which have come to him from others. Schiller also asserts that the Shingon sect greatly surpasses all other sects, for example, Shin, Jōdō, Zen, and Hokke. Reischauer calls Kūkai a "perverter of Buddhism"[41], whose, "clever compromise with Shintoism" lets no good light fall upon him. One may indeed even raise the question of whether the Protestant conception of the "homo religiousus" really applies to the Daishi, or whether there is not in him all too much of that magician who through the power of his prayers and invocations, of his sacrifices and other practices to supernatural powers, desires to attain the rule over the animate as well as over the inanimate world. Indeed, magic prayers, the kaji-prayers, play a great role in Kōbō's cult; he himself employed them repeatedly. To give only one example, according to the biography by his disciple Shinzei, he built

---

[41] Reischauer, "Studies in Japanese Buddhism", p99 (Translator's note)

a prayer-altar for the sake of the country not less than fifty-one times, and successfully produced rain or warded off storm, sickness, and so forth, by prayer. I do not possess enough knowledge of theology to decide the question by entering into a comparative study of the teaching of Kūkai and that of other great founders of Japanese religions, such as Hōnen, Shinran, and Nichiren. Kūkai is the embodiment to a high degree of the whole spiritual tendency of his time, in which the religious and the magical were inseparably connected. In China this tendency was held in check at the court, and could not have established itself so quickly in Japan in spite of all the merits of the master if it had not been, so to speak, in the air.

I should like to consider only two or three additional points. In the first place, of Kūkai's five brothers and sisters, two brothers became known as priests, Shiaga Sōjō and Shinnen Daitoku[42], while the son of his older sister became known as Chisen Daitoku, and the son of younger sister, Chishō Daishi, even became one of the patriarchs of the Tendai sect. There must therefore have prevailed in the family a strong leaning toward religion, as well as statesmanlike and military traits. As for the reproach of a lack of originality, even the person of the founder of the Buddhist

---

[42] Daitoko or ōtoko is the most correct pronunciation, but one used very little nowadays.

teaching cannot properly speaking be acquitted wholly of this blemish. Those greatest in the field of literature, a Moliere, a Shakespeare, have had to put up with it. The question is: "Has Kōbō taken over blindly and imitated slavishly what he saw and learned in China, or are there not shown many times in his whole work a free disposal of the good which he has taken over, a completely sovereign control of all he has learned and acquired, and a practice of the same, which is just as original in its way? In contrast to Schiller, Lloyd designates Kūkai's system of teaching as an innovation, no matter whence it may have been derived.

Reischauer calls him a "perverter of Buddhism" chiefly on account of his magic, but even if we grant the justice of his reproach, it is not concerned with Kūkai, but with Asamga (in Japanese: *Mujaku Bosatsu*), who worked long before him, and through whom first, according to investigations up to the present time, the magic element crept into Buddhism. For the rest, we meet here the as yet unsettled province of the authenticity of Mahayana Buddhism, a field in which I am not competent to judge. As for the compromise between Buddhism and Shintoism – or better, the synthesis of the two-, this redounds to the credit of Kōbō Daishi even today, according to many Japanese authorities, for example, Tomita. The later development of his teaching relating to this matter showed various outgrowths, but for the common people Ryōbu Shinto, as the teaching is commonly called today, appears to have great advantages. To wish to foist upon Kūkai in this connection the desire for political power seems from my point of view to understand the master's personality.[43] The fundamental thought of Ryōbu Shinto, the identification of the Japanese kami and the (Buddhist) *hotoke*, corresponds throughout the whole system of the secret teaching of Shingon with its constant transit from synthesis to antithesis, and from this again to synthesis.

That the Shingon sect is surpassed today by all other great sects is an assertion for which I could find no confirmation. It is surpassed only the Shin sect, which works in every respect with the most modern methods, and by the Zen sect; but in recent years it appears to have progressed rather than to have retreated. In Shikoku it stands at the head of all sects. In order to form a picture of the influence which it still has today, consider the fact that only lately strikes in Osaka have been settled many times through calling in of the Arch-abbot of Koya-san as a mediator.

Concerning the significance of Kūkai in general, I should like to quote Lloyd, who writes as follows in regard to the legends about the Daishi, "It is certain that many of the legends which have attached themselves to the person

---

[43] Compare the warning in his will not to lead Koya-san into political (…text cut off)

of the Saint are false. But the fact that so many legends have gathered around him, and that even today the worshippers of this sect worship, no Vairocana pure and simple, but Vairocana incarnated in Kōbō Daishi, shows us that we are here in the presence of some great man. Legend does not adhere to mediocrity; it is only genius that can keep the popular imagination centred in itself." Dr. T. Tanimoto (1867-1946) in his 1922 book, *Nippon Bunka to Bukkyo* (Japanese Culture and Buddhism, p.166), also comes to the same conclusion, although he credits a part of the legends as being fact, as for example, that Kūkai more than any other person before or after him had wandered around the country, and therefore had left behind him an especially enduring impression upon the people. But even so, only a truly great man could have left behind such an impression. He who could so set in motion the religious fancy of a people as Kūkai succeeded in doing must have attained to a strong religious power. I have certainly seen on my journey such superstition and the like, of which I shall speak later: everywhere behind Tokushima the mountains were smoking with the burnt-offerings of those who, like Kūkai once, were praying for rain. But on the whole I received the impression that Kūkai's spirit and influence today after 1100 years are still living in such a way that one would find it difficult to think of this persistent influence an emanating from a man who had not been a strong religious personality. This influence is so powerful that it extends even to temples and adherents of wholly different sects.

II. Origin of the Pilgrimage

The influence emanating from Kūkai and enduring for well over a thousand years appears more wonderful if we ask ourselves the question, "How did the pilgrimage originate?" and thereby stumble at the outset upon the fact that from only three of the temples do we have proof from authentic historical documents the Kūkai stayed at them. Of these three, one lies in Awa (Tairyu-ji, No.21), one in Tosa (Higashi-dera, No.24), and one in Sanuki (Zentsū-ji, No.75), while up to the present time we have no record of any kind to prove that the master ever visited the fourth province, Iyo, from which, according to legend, there nevertheless came the impulse to go on pilgrimage, and which today can show more pilgrimage temples than any one of the other three provinces. In the oldest biographies, even in those written within the first 250 years after his death, we find not the least hint of the institution of a pilgrimage to the 88 holy places of Shikoku. Occasional mention of the pilgrimage is found in other books rather early, but the oldest book that informs us about its origin is *Shikoku Henrei Kudoku-ki* (Chronicles of the Miraculous

Power of the Shikoku Pilgrimage). This book appeared in the third years of Genroku (1690) and contains in two large illustrated volumes some statements about the origin and the significance of the journey, some records of miraculous cures, and some legends from the Daishi's life.

The author of the book has three things to say about the origin of the pilgrimage:

1. Who began the pilgrimage, and when, is not possible to say definitely.

2. There is a tale, according to which Kūkai's disciple Shinzei after his master's death visited in remembrance some of the places where the latter had labored during his lifetime. Others followed his example, and so the custom of pilgrimage arose.

3. According to another version, after Kūkai's death his spirit sought out the places of his former activity and hovered over them in a cloud. News of this spread, and it gradually came about that more and more people set out on the pilgrimage in order to meet the Daishi.

This last version we can consign to the realm of legend without further comment. With regard to the first, we may remark that later research has already cleared up much that appeared at first impossible of discovery. As far as the second version is concerned, there is nothing in the story itself to make us reject it. To be sure, we find in Shinzei's biography no hint of a visit to Shikoku. There is mention only of the fact that in the 11ᵗʰ year of Kōnin (820) he accompanied his master to the Kantō area. It would have been quite possible; however, for Shinzei to have visited the places reminding him of his highly honoured teacher, and for other disciples, many of whom, by the way, came from Shikoku, to have followed his example, a circumstance from which the custom of going on pilgrimage might gradually have come. But even if we accept this explanation, it still remains very improbable the fixing of the number 88 took places at such an early time.

This would seem to be the right point in our discussion to complete some remarks made in the introduction about the origin of the custom of going on pilgrimage, and to see if we cannot find some further traces of the origin of the life of pilgrimage in Japan, even though we accept as the chief reasons those mentioned above. First comes the question, whether the indigenous religion, Shinto, is concerned in any way with the flourishing of the custom of pilgrimage. I have not succeeded in discovering any connections worth mentioning in this respect. To be sure, there are isolated mountains, for example, the Ko no Mine (No.27) in Tosa, where Shinto divinities were reverenced before the founding of the Buddhist temple. But their number is soon exhausted. With the exception of the above mentioned Ko no Mine, only the temple Kakurin-ji (No.20), lying on a high mountain, and Tairyu-ji (No.21), and perhaps also No.41,47,60 and 74 can be cited. At the rest of the temples the connections with Shinto all seem to arise from a later period, the hey-day of Ryōbu Shinto. Even where there are Shinto pilgrimages today, for example, that in Matsuyama to the eight shrines on the outskirts of the city, the so-called *hasshamōde*, famous in ancient times, they are all of a more recent date. The only indication that I found of anything that could be called a "journey around" was in an article of the Encyclopaedia Japonica, which explained the origin of the designation Ichi no Miya. The account there ran that in the Nara Period the rulers of the separate districts (*kokushi*) had to visit yearly certain shrines that could boast of an ancient origin and had something like an official status in their provinces. Shinto can therefore have contributed to the development of the spirit of pilgrimage only so far as worship of nature and of mountain tops played a role in it.

It is quite otherwise with those two great forerunners of Kūkai, Gyogi Bosatsu and En no Ozunu.[44] Gyogi Bosatsu, who lived between 670 and 749, travelled through the greater part of the 60 provinces of the realm after the death of his mother, preaching and founding temples everywhere. A great number of the Shikoku temples trace

---

[44] The reading of the names runs thus in the oldest documents. Today one is accustomed to read "En no Shōkaku", provided one does not choose the designation En no Gyōja (that is, En the Anchorite).

their origin back to this great wandering preacher, who has, moreover, points of contact with Kōbō Daishi also in the case of Ryobu Shinto; for although the union of Buddhism and Shintoism belongs to a later time, the first beginnings emanated from Gyogi. We may well assume that many a priest, and perhaps also many a layman, followed Gyogi's example, but as founder and promoter of the custom of going on pilgrimage En no Ozunu of the previous generation had a much greater significance. He was born in the year 635 in the province of Yamato, was a zealous adherent of the Buddhist teaching from his early youth on, and as a religious practice climbed the highest mountain peaks of his home province and the province of Kii. At the age of 32 he was the first to climb Mount Ibaragi, and for more than thirty years he lived there in a rock cave, where he practiced the teaching of Kujaku Myōō.[45] In his later years he journeyed through the western part of Japan as far as Kyushu. The year of his death is unknown; he appears, however, to have reached a ripe old age. According to one version, he is said finally to have journeyed to China.

---

[45] *Kujaku Myōō*, the Clear Luminōs Peacock King, is a Buddhist image with one head and four arms, which is depicted riding a peacock. There are also representations in which the figure is only holding a peacock in his hand. In spite of the fact that the title, *Myōō*, "Clear Luminous King", is given only to those terror-arousing divinities like Fudō who subdue evil spirits, Kujaku Myōō is no terror-awakening figure, but is even designated as Buddha's mother.

The teaching of En no Ozunu is Shugendo. The heart of the teaching does not differ greatly from the *mikkyo* of the Shingon and the Tendai sects, and after the Restoration, Shugendo was even incorporated in both these sects. What is especially remarkable, however, is the worship of mountain peaks. Omine-san near Yoshino was designated by En no Ozunu as the holy of holies of his teaching, but it appears that for about 180 years after Ozunu's death the ascent of mountains (*nyūbu*, literally, treading of the peak) was discontinued, and was first taken up again by the Shingon priest Shōbō, known subsequently as Rigen Daishi. It was Rigen Daishi who recognized the secret teaching of Ozunu as allied to Shingon and therefore incorporated it in the latter. The name Shugendo is explained as abbreviation of *Shugyō tokuken dō*, that is *Kujakuō-juhō-wo shugyō shite igenryoku wo eru michi* (= a way to attain to special miraculous power through the practice of the magic teaching of the Peacock King). Since in their religious practice the adherents of this teaching had to spend most of their nights out-of-doors in mountains, which were at that time still uninhabited, they were also called *yamabushi* (yama=mountain, fusu=to rest, to lie); therefore, this name became later of theological significance, and for *fusu* another another character was chosen which signified "to lie, to lurk", so that yamabushi came to be interpreted as the "the persons waylaying (error) from the mountain (truth)." Through the influence of Rigen Daishi, Shugendo became very popular among persons of both high and low rank, and gradually a special costume grew up, so that in the Tokugawa era we have an equipment not only fixed in all details but even with a theological explanation for every part (see note to p. 137). It is remarkable to note that the staff that, as we shall see, occupies so important a place in the Shikoku pilgrimage, plays a comparatively subordinate role in Shugendo. Today the teaching has two branches, of which the larger is called Honzanha and is connected with the Tendai Sect, while the smaller known as Tozanha belongs to the Shingon Sect. The adherence of the latter branch climb Mount Omine three times yearly and say their prayers in the holy of holies for the good fortune and the peace of realm (*Tenka Taihei no Kitō*), while the adherents of the Honzan Sect do this only once a year.

There is no doubt that Shugendo has helped in large measure to develop the practice of going on pilgrimage, even if this teaching never came into full flower on Shikoku. To give only one example, the equipment of the Shikoku pilgrim has never become as symbolic as that of the yamabushi, but, as we can see from the old pictures, has always remained more adapted to the real needs of the pilgrims. Nevertheless, the connection between them is not wholly lacking. For lack of historical documents we are again referred to simple tradition, but according to that it appears that En no Oznunu also visited Shikoku. Thus, Temple No.12, Shōsan-ji, situated high in the mountains in Awa, traces the founding of its holy of holies (*okunoin*) to him; in Tosa he is said to have exorcised mountain spirits at the 38th temple, the "Foot Stamp Mountain", so that they could only stamp powerlessly with their feet; likewise, the 47th temple, Yasaka-ji, not far from Matsuyama, is said to have been founded by him, while the 43rd temple, Akeshi-ji, names its founder Jugen Sonja, an ancestor of Ozunu's of five generations before him. Even the Buddhist incarnation of the Shinto divinity of the highest mountain in Shikoku, Zōō Gongen, worshipped at two temples, the 60th and the 64th, is the reincarnation of Shaka Nyorai, which revealed itself for the first time to En no Ozunu on Mount Kinpu in the province of Yamato, and appears neither in India nor in China. Yet Mount Ishizuchi was climbed for the first time in the year 850 by a priest, and at that time the divinity of the mountain was worshipped as Zōō Gongen.[46] En no Ozunu himself is said to have carved the image of Zōō Gongen in the 64th temple, according to a guidebook from as long ago as the Bunkwa era (1804-1818).

The question as to whether Taoism has anything to do with the rise of the Shikoku pilgrimage cannot be decided because of a complete lack of source material. While

---

[46] The Shinto divinity is Ishizuchi Hiko no Mikoto.

we at least have tradition of Gyogi and En no Ozunu, nothing has come down to us concerning any connection with Taoism. To be sure, the mountain peaks in groups of five, characteristic of this religion, appear several times: at Zentsu-ji, the temple of Kūkai's birth, where the *Gogaku*, the five knolls arise[47]; at the 85th temple, which on account of the five jagged mountains[48] rising in the background is called *Gokenzon* (Five Sword Mountain); yet again, at the 71st temple, Kengozan (Sword Five Mountain); and at the 31st temple, which lies upon one of five mountains rising in undulations, and is therefore called *Godaisan* (Five Summit Mountain). That an influence through Taoism is not to be denied of itself, one sees through the fact that a Buddhist scholar already cited, Professor Tomita, expresses a conjecture along this line (Shikoku Henro p45, line 2, ff).

Summarizing, we can therefore say that the custom of going on pilgrimage, as already noted in the introduction, came to Japan from India through China; that, in addition to early wandering preachers, such as Gyogi Bosatsu, En no Ozunu and the adherents of his teaching may be considered the chief awakeners of the spirit of pilgrimage among the Japanese, even if their influence has

---

[47] With reference to these, the biography translated by Schiller is called "Gogaku no Kumo." (The Clouds of the Five Knolls)
[48] The photograph of this district in the book on Japan by Trautz (p199) is unfortunately taken from a side which does not allow one to distinguish the five points.

been less strong in Shikoku. Although the Shikoku pilgrimage cannot be traced back to Kōbō Daishi himself as the founder, but rather goes back to the Saikoku pilgrimage as a model, there is nevertheless no doubt that Kōbō Daishi's inclination to mountain-top Buddhism received its first and strongest stimulation from the mountain temples of Shikoku. It is also not outside the bounds of probability that, with the attempts soon after Kūkai's death of the city- and palace- Buddhism in Kyoto to suppress the mountain-top Buddhism of Koya-san, Mukū, and other priests devoted to the latter way abandoned Koya-san, turned to Shikoku, and there nourished the original teaching. We shall allude once more to this point in another connection (see p62), and will content ourselves here with this brief allusion.

III. Characteristics of the pilgrimage, oldest documents and books, descriptions of the journey

We have said above that the definite fixing of the number of temples at 88 could scarcely have proceeded from Kūkai himself. On the contrary, there is first of all the fact that the oldest documents referring to the pilgrimage speak only of the way of the Shikoku district (*Shikoku henro*), out of which there comes later "Shikoku Circular Road" (Shikoku henro; *hen* written with another charac-

74

ter).[49] That the name henro, which today has become universal as a designation for pilgrims, must already have been the customary expression in the mouths of the common people long before the first books about the pilgrimage appeared, one sees from the fact that although in the oldest books the characters henrei are written, the furigana "henro" are written beside them. A variation of henro in dialect is *hendo*, a fact which had led Professor Kida (Kyoto) to the false assumption that *hendo* is the original, and that it came from *hen* (round) and *do* (country). Yet *hendo* (pilgrim) is nowhere to be found written in this way. When one wants to represent the form in dialect in writing today, he uses either the kana characters or the facetious transcription *hen* (one-sided, odd) and *do* (fellow). The only example which Professor Kida gives in support of his thesis is a place in the Kamakura-ki of the Abbot Takuan: "*Jōchiji ni irite mireba sangen shimen no dō ichiu furuki hotoke wo anchi shite doko wo kaisantō to iubeki yō mo naku matsuryū hendo no sō hitori kitariete, katsukatsu bōoku chiisaku itonami katawera ni ari….*" (When I entered the temple Jōchi, I fōnd a hall six meters square, in which an old image of Buddha was set up. Nowhere was there anything that could serve as a building in memory of the founder. A *hendo* priest of

---

[49] Other expressions are today; "O-Shikoku meguri", "O Shikoku-mawari", "O Shikoku-sama", and somewhat more politely, "Go Junrei", "Go Jumpai."

low priest was there; on one side was a little hut poorly built…) As Professor Kageura, whom I follow in the main in the above discussion, proves by various documents, it is impossible that a pilgrim is meant by *hendo*. It means rather "rural, rustic", and is still preserved today in the dialect of the neighbourhood of Yamagoe in Iyo with this significance. Also, the assumption of Bukkyō Daijiten that henro has come from *henrei* is to be rejected after what has been said above. That a very old book, the *Konjaku Monogatari* (Stories of Then and Now) by Takakuni Minamoto, who died in 1077, speaks of "Shikoku Henchi (or Henji)", could according to Kageura very well be an error of Minamoto, depending upon an interchange of *chi, ji* (earth) with *ro* (way), which also has the reading *ji*. Summing up, we may therefore say with Kageura that in ancient times the designation henro was the correct one, which was later replaced by henro and henro (with a different writing of hen in each case); when, then, this word had become the general term for a pilgrim, a new designation henrei was given to the pilgrimage. So the oldest guidebook that gives the temples in their present order directs the pilgrim to write on his ticket:

"Osametatematsuru Henrei Shikokuchū Reijō Dōgyō Futari"
(Pilgrimage to the Holy Places of Shikokūnder-

taken in reverence by two travelling companions)

The fact, however, that the furigana "henro" are written beside the characters henrei shows, as already noted, that the latter is still the usual expression. Still later arose the designation *junrei*, or the expression that is used the most today:

> "Shikoku Hachijūhakkasho Reijō Junpai Dōgyō Futari"

While the earlier from has been preserved until the present time in the inscription on the ticket-box.

The number 88 is mentioned from the first time on a temple gong (*waniguchi*) dating from the third year of Bunmei (1471) that is in the Jizō-dō of the village of Motokawa, Tosa District, Tosa Province. The inscription is badly weather-beaten, and part of it is no longer legible. It mentions four names, two of men and two of women, who are designated as *ōdanna*, which is representatives of a Buddhist parish. It might therefore be possible that even at that time there were group pilgrimages and pilgrimages by proxy (daisan: see p. 261).[50] In the book Uwa Kyūki that came out somewhat later but cannot be dated exactly, the following is written in the paragraph on Inari Daimyōjin

---

[50] The inscription, untranslatable because of the gaps in it, is cited by Kageura, p138.

(the present No. 41): "Shikoku Hachijūhakkasho no ikka-sho nari." (It is one of the 88 places of Shikoku).

The first *fuda*, the name-ticket of a pilgrim, is preserved for us from the third year of Kei-an (1650). It is at the shrine of the chief divinity of Enmyō-ji (No.53), in the village of Wake near Matsuyama, is made of copper, and in contrast to those commonly used today in Shikoku is slanted off at the top.[51] The inscription runs:

Kei-an sannen   Kyōgoku
Osametatematsuru Shikokuehū Henro Dōgyō Futari
Dōgetsu Dōjitsu   Keijin Iyetsugi

Third year of Kei-an   Kyōgoku (place of residence in Kyoto)
Pilgrimage thrōgh Shikokūnderstaken in reverence by two travelling companions
The same month, the same day   Citizen Iyetsugi

Here again the statement of number is lacking, but it may be assumed from the details that it has to do with one of the 88 temples. That is my personal conviction, and I also believe that the temple gong represents the sacrificial gift

---

51 Editor – It is interesting that Bohner does not mention Frederick Starr's claimed discovery of this fuda during his pilgrimage in 1921, six years previous to Bohner.

of one or more pilgrims, since it as well as the ticket has March as the designation of the month, and even to the present day this has been the month in which most of the pilgrims make the pilgrimage. That the words, "Pilgrimage through Shikoku" stand upon the ticket (without designation of number) is explained by the fact that the chief thing is the pilgrimage through Shikoku, and the limitation of this pilgrimage, or, which is equally possible, its explanation, to 88 temples took place later on.

In other books up to the 16th Century we find only isolated references to the Shikoku temples, but in the 15th year of Kan-ei (1638) we have the first description of a pilgrim journey, no less a one than that of an Imperial prince, Kūchō Hōshinnō, written by him by Kenmyō, the abbot of Sugōzan (No.44). Yet this description is confined to letting a poetical note sound at this or that temple or historical scene, in the 7-5-7-5 meter of the Buddhist songs of worship (*was an*), while the content set forth in such a charmingly witty and playful fashion is somewhat brief, and unfortunately we learn practically nothing about the experiences of the prince and the conditions of those times. The first ten temples are dismissed with the short verse, "*Jūri jikkasho achisugite*", without even their names being given. In contrast to this, the landscape near Matsuyama is described in detail. The book can therefore scarcely be regarded as a source.[52]

Toward the end of the Jōkyō era (1684-1688) and at the beginning of the Genroku era (1688-1704) there appeared at one time a succession of books that were concerned exclusively with our pilgrimage, most of them written by the priests of Koya-san. They were designed for the use of pilgrims and were therefore written in a style approaching the colloquial language and easily understood.

The oldest is *Shikokudō Shi-nan* (Guidebook to the Shikoku way) by Shinnen, a priest of Koya-san, written in the third year of Genroku (1688).[53] The book contains in the introduction advice and instructions for pilgrims, cost and conditions of travel for the journey by sea from Osaka to the ports of Shikoku, and so forth; then it describes the way from temple to temple, following the order used today. It

---

[52] Editor – It is claimed by Komatsu Katsuki that this book was not written in 1638, but the late Meiji period and 1925. (See Ehime University Pilgrimage Conference Proceedings, 2008. P.22-32)

[53] Editor – Actual name of the book *Shikoku Michishirube*. Translator – It may seem as though this had appeared rather late, but if we compare with it the books about the Saikoku pilgrimage, it is apparent that the oldest book on the 33 Kwannon temples, the Saikoku Meisho-ki of the 8th year of Enpo, is only six years older. While, however, several books on the Shikoku pilgrimage appeared in the Genroku Era, further works on the Saikoku pilgrimage did not appear until the 11th year of Kyoho (1726) and still later, in the 5th year of An-ei (1776).

also includes, as do modern guidebooks, the image of the chief divinity of each temple, though in somewhat larger and more beautiful form, and then some more information, for example, the direction of the heavens towards which the chief building faces, as well as some illustrations, among which the wild horses upon the moon between Usa and Susaki (Tosa) and view from Misaka Pass over Matsuyama and the Japan Inland Sea are especially good. A number of legends are scattered through it, and the landscape here and there is described, the district around Kume, now well built-up, being pictured as wildly romantic. The author pauses for a rather long time at the hotspring bath in Dogo.[54] To the practical counsel that the book gives the pilgrim belongs, for example, the advice to provide oneself at a given spot with everything needed,

---

[54] "Since the time of the Emperor Keiko, princes of various families have visited the bath at Dogo, as may be perceived from the Nihongi. Under the rule of the Empress Suikō, the Crown Prince Shotoku also deigned to come here. The bathing pools of Dogo of which the Genji Monogatari speaks are here. There are five basins for bathing. The first is the *Kagiyu* (perhaps falsely written by the author, who was not familiar with the place, for *Kami no yu*, still in existence today, since it agrees with the description) into which ordinary people may not go. In this bath there is a stone figure of Yakushi, at whose feet the hot water gushes forth like a waterfall. The second bath is designed for women, the third for men, the fourth is called 'Life Dispensing Bath' (*Yōjō*). Guests come continually to the bath day and night, from all provinces, men and women in equal numbers. Into the fifth bath go the *eta* (outcasts) as well as horses and oxen...."

since for the next stretch of such-and-such a length nothing can be bought; or the information where and how the necessary entrance papers may be made out at the border of each new province; or even the instruction to give up one's ticket for the 37th temple at the ferry across the river in case of high water, since it would then be impossible to cross.[55] It is also asserted in one place in the book that the highest mountain in Shikoku, Mount Ishizuchi, is open at the beginning of the sixth month of each year for only three days of climbing. The three iron chains, which today form a part of the climb, are first mentioned in the Bunkwa era.

A second book, *Shikoku Reijō-ki* (Chronicles of the holy places of Shikoku, seven volumes) dates likewise from the beginning of the Genroku era. The author, Jakuhon, a priest of Koya-san, mentions in his preface *Shikokudō Shi-nan*, which he considers lacking in detail and will therefore enlarge upon. For each temple he gives a sketch showing the situation and the arrangement of the buildings. The text is also enlarged, and the description of the road more exact.

The third book, *Shikoku Henrei Kudoku-ki* (Chronicle of the Miraculous Power of the journey around Shikoku),

---

[55] On my pilgrimage I came after a great downpour of rain to one place where the signboard pointed unmistakably up the bed of a river in which muddy waters, deep as a man is tall, were rolling along. Fortunately, someone directed me to a bridge about half a mile downstream, so that I did not need to interrupt my journey.

dates from the 3rd year of Genroku (1690) and consists of two small volumes. It is occupied somewhat, as we saw above, with the origin of the pilgrimage, and then introduces some stories of miraculous cures as well as some legends, which the oldest book also contains. The ideas for the numerous wood-cuts are partly borrowed from the *Shikokudō Shi-nan*.

The above-named books were all somewhat expensive for that time: The seven-volume set cost, for example, 5 monne of silver (about 2/3 of an ounce). For less fat purses, I found, however, a little book advertised in *Shikokudō Shi-nan, Shikoku Henri Michishirube* (Guide for the Shikoku pilgrimage), whose price was fixed, surely not by chance, at 88 mon (less than one sen of present-day currency).

Another book, *Kōbō Daishi Sangi-ho* (A Contribution to the Praise and the Understanding of Kōbō Daishi, 3 small volumes), is also advertised in the Shikokudō Shi-nan, but I was unable to obtain a copy of this book.

In the year 1747 there appeared the first attempt at a map of the pilgrimage, *Shikoku Henrei-zu* (Map, or rather, Picture of the Shikoku Pilgrimage). The author, Keifu (or Kyōfu) Hosoda, regrets the fact that there is no pictorial representation of the Shikoku pilgrim journey, and sets himself the task of supplying the lack.

In any case, the old books are very difficult to procure, since they were usually (and still are) put with the pilgrim into his coffin together with the book of written offerings and – at least in the neighbourhood of Matsuyama – with a small volume of hymns of the 33 Kwannon temples.

We shall have frequent occasion later to mention the conservatism that governs the whole pilgrimage. It appears also if we compare the books mentioned above, especially *Shikokudō Shi-nan*, with later works. On the whole, the plan remains the same: large sections of the earlier books are incorporated word for word in the later ones, the only difference being that the newer books omit more and more of the decorative accessories, such as legends or detailed descriptions of landscapes, and confine themselves more closely to their peculiar task of guide and vadenecum. A guidebook from the Bunkwa era (1804-1818) and one from the Tempo era (1830-1844) that were at my disposal in the writing of this book agree in general with the old one from the Jokyo era (1684-1688), yet there is already a lack of certain places in which the landscape is described, as far as such description does not directly concern the condition of the road. One or another of the legends is also omitted, even though as a whole they are taken over unchanged. The guidebook of today (for the title see Bibliography, p. 275) has, on the contrary, no more of these legends, unless they have a direct reference to the founding of a temple. The introductory section, treating of preparation for the journey, equipment, and so forth, has on the other hand become more detailed with the passage of time. Above all, the present-day guidebook gives the exact prayers that the pilgrim has to say at each temple. Today, therefore, the description of the road, the determination of the distance, information about possibilities of shelter, and so forth, are more exact; statements about founders and restorers of the holy places are – perhaps at the cost of historical accuracy – more complete. But the book of today still has the loops of the pack thread printed on its cover.

An exception is a book that appeared in the Matsuyama in the 28th year of the Meiji era (1895) and bears the title *Koseki Yūran Shikoku Meisho-ki* (Guidebook to the Inspection of the Historical Monuments and to the Sights of Shikoku; briefly, An Historical Guidebook to the Shikoku). This book was thought of also as a guidebook for the pilgrimage, but gives in addition in its nearly 350 pages a profusion of information about other temples, battlefields, and historical places, quoting from old sources beginning with the Kojiki and the Nihongi, and paying special attention to the province of Iyo. Besides four copper-plate engravings we find a list of over 800 books dealing in some way with Shikoku. It is a shame, however, that credible material and doubtful material are placed uncritically side by side in the book, and since the __ of the author have sold as wastepaper all the valuable old books and documents that he possessed and used, it is possible in most cases to confirm the information contained in the book.

The newest in the field of guidebooks literature consists in an Agricultural Guidebook along the Route of the Shikoku Pilgrimage, published in September, 1929, by the agricultural associations of the four provinces, with the object of bringing to the attention of those pilgrims interested in agricultural problems the things worth seeing, especially the numerous model projects carried on by the associations.

Besides the book of Prince Kūshō, only three real book of travel have come to my attention, and I shall refer to them later several times.

I. *Shikoku Henrei Dōgyō Futari*, by Shikoku-zaru[56], pseudonym for Kikutarō Kan, at present professor in the agricultural school in Matsuyama; published in 1903 in the Tokyo newspaper, Niroku Shimbun." This description gives many interesting observations. Regarding the mira-

[56] Shikoku-zaru, ie. Shikoku Ape, is a nickname that might well have come from the fact that in earlier times many monkey-men (Translator's note: men travelling with monkeys and earning their living by exhibiting the tricks of the animals) came from Shikoku, chiefly from Awa. The name is given to the inhabitants of Shikoku to designate them as smallish people, with little originality, only skillful in imitation of others.

cles of the Daishi, the author shows himself to be somewhat skeptical, and gives his own rational explanations.
The language is remarkable for the strong mixture of the
style of that period with Chinese expressions, which has
almost passed out of use today.

II. *Shikoku Henro Dōgyō Futari*, by Kanikumo, professor for Shinohara, at that time editor of the newspaper,
Ehime Shimpo, in Matsuyama, in whose columns the description appeared between September and November,
1926. The author makes many criticisms of social conditions – he later became a member of the Labor Movement,
gives many very coarse interludes, and finally abandons
the journey, since he has become weary of it.

III. *Shikoku Henro*, by Kōjun Tomita, professor at the
Buddhist Higher School, Taishō Daigaku, in Tokyo, and
priest of the Hōsen-ji on the outskirts of the capital. The
little book appeared in Tokyo in November, 1926. It is
written, like the other descriptions, in the form of a diary,
and is especially instructive because it pictures the observations of a priest, and gives many points of view.

B. The temples

I. Number and Distribution over the Four Provinces.

The Four Stages of Faith

There are various theories regarding the fixing of the number of the temples at 88. The most probable is the one that states that the 88 temples represent the affiliations of the senses, the 88 passions.[57] As the pilgrim goes from temple to temple and carries out his religious practices, he becomes free from these passions, one after the other, and returns home purified, if, as Kanikumo wickedly remarks, the first ones have not meanwhile attacked him anew, before he has become free of the eight-and-eightieth. Another explanation commonly accepted by Buddhist theologians is that while he was in China Kōbō Daishi received some earth from each of the eight famous Buddhist temples in India, used it in founding eight temples in Shikoku, decided to found ten times that number of temples in addition, and so introduced the pilgrimage. This theory, however, takes it for granted that Kūkai was really the founder of the pilgrimage, an assumption that, as we have already seen, is not upheld by the facts of history. It might

---

[57] Generally one speaks not of 88 but of 108 passions, and therefore a modern guidebook chooses 20 of the worthiest of the numerous *bangai* (temples lying outside the regular round) in order to reach this number.

rather be possible that besides the explanation given first above the idea of the ideograph for rice, which, when separated into its component parts, becomes 88, had some influence on the fixing of the number of the temples. This explanation fits into the picture so much the better since many pilgrims write on their tickets the prayer, "Prosperity of the five kinds of grain", among which rice of course the most important. Finally, the theory that 88 represents the sum of the dangerous ages of man, woman, and child (42-37-9, or 42-33-15) is worthy of special notes, because it show the penetration of European ideas, since the conception of 13[58] as an unlucky number was originally unknown to the Japanese.

Today the journey begins at Reisan-ji in Bandō near Tokushima.[59] This is the order of pilgrimage prescribed in the oldest books extant. It is based upon the fact that Kūkai

---

[58] That 13 is considered an unlucky number in ever-widening circles today is shown by the example of the Ishizaki Steamship Company, whose ships ply between Mitsuhama near Matsuyama, Onomichi, and Ujima. After the steamer "Aioi-Maru No. 12", No. 15 was built, since 13 and 14 betoken misfortune, 14 on account of the number 4, which has the same pronunciation as *shi* (death).

[59] This is the place known to many Germans whose relatives were brought as prisoners to the parade ground in the neighbourhood after the fall of Tsingtao in the year 1918. The band of the Marine Battalion of Tsingtao has played more than once in Reisan-ji. (Editor – The proper reading is Ryozen-ji)

coming form his visit to the Tairyu-ji of Kyoto landed here and started his journey inland. Nevertheless, this order could not have fixed absolutely before the Genroku era, since the Shikoku Reijo-ki of only a few years later requests that the pilgrimage be began at the birthplace of Kūkai, the present Zentsū-ji. Even if this request could not be granted, and one reckons today from Reisan-ji on through the provinces of Awa, Tosa, Iyo and Sanuki, naming Ookubo-ji in the last named province as the final temple, the place of the fulfillment of the vow, this numbering is not binding, either. For no pilgrim is obliged to make the pilgrimage strictly in this order, nor to begin it at any particular temple; he may even leave out some temples and visit them later. He can begin at any temple that he likes, and may even make the pilgrimage in reverse order. The bodily and spiritual gain, promised to the believer is not in the least curtailed thereby.

Distribution over the several provinces is as follows:

Awa (present name – Tokushima) No. 1-23   23 temples
Tosa (present name – Kōchi)   No. 24-30 16 temples
Iyo (present name- Ehime)   No.40-65   26 temples
Sanuki (present name – Kagawa) No. 66-88 23 temples.

In regard to this distribution, there is an edifying explanation in poetic form, according to which each of the four provinces represents one of the four states of faith: Hosshin, Shugyō, Bodai, and Nehan (the creation of belief in the heart, practice in conduct, awakening, Nirvana)

AWA

In Awa the temples, especially the first ten, lie closest together. From the first to the tenth stretch scarely six *ri* (24 kilometers), so that the inhabitants of that region call the journey up to and back from these temples a day's pilgrimage. One goes up by the valley of the Yoshino through pleasant mulberry groves. None of the first ten lies especially high. After one has enjoyed once more the beautiful view from No.10, Kirihata-ji, over the valley of the Yoshino River and the blue mountains, he crosses in a ferry over the river, whose bed at this point is almost 900 meters wide[60] and soon reaches the 11th temple. The 12th temple, Shōsan-ji lies a considerable height, 600-700 meters, but the succeeding temples are again all on rather level ground. We go down the valley, swing around Tokushima, the capital of the province, and after we have visited this temple where the grave of Kūkai's mother is – Onzan-ji, with its mountain cemetery, which arouses deep emotion -, we draw near the coast not far from Komatsushima. From the 19th temple, Tatsue-ji, we again go into the mountains.

---

[60] The stream of water itself is not as wide, but it is very clear, with a depth of six to seven meters.

Moreover, the succeeding temples lie somewhat farther apart, but as one leads a child from the easier to the harder, the pilgrim too becomes gradually accustomed to effort; he has learned the songs and the prayers, and in addition he is rewarded for the difficulties of the road at the 20th temple and at the 21st, Tairyū-ji, by the sight of magnificent temple buildings of such perfection and in such enchanting accord with Nature as he will find again in but few temples of the journey. Everywhere along the way fresh springs refresh him; between Kakurin-ji and Tairyū-ji the beautiful valley of the Naka River revives him; behind Tairyū-ji he passes with dread by the great stalactite cave of the island, the Dragon Cave, from whose interior there comes forth an icy breath, while the roaring of the torrent eddying past his feet is re-echoed a hundred comes from the walls gleaming moistly in the light of the flickering candles. The road leads on through pleasant valleys, where gentle hands serve him tea, and when finally the huge mirror of the Pacific Ocean shines before his eyes and he has climbed the stone steps of Yakuō-ji at Hiwasa, and looks upon the neat little town and the harbour, the Kotsu Bodaishin, the awakening of the believing heart, has been completed in him.

TOSA

But now, as he gets ready to visit Tosa, the scene changes suddenly. The landscape stretches out endlessly long, and with it the road along the coast of the ocean. The holy places are fews, and one must often pass a whole day, or even several days, before he comes to one again. From Yakuō-ji to the next temple he must pass over more than 20 ri (80 kilometers). The road to Tosa accounts for more than a third of the pilgrimage, although the 16 temples of the province make up less than a fifth of the whole number. Moreover, the journey here was in earlier days tremendously hard. In one place the road even stopped completely on the rocky coast, and for a certain distance one had to walk with garments held high over stones that, washed by the breakers in this ever-restless part of the sea, threatened at the least misstep to slip, and to plunge the careless pilgrim into a salt bath. *"Tobiishi, haneishi, gorogoroishi"* (jumping stones, spring stones, rolling stones) they called these dangerous places. Today Tosa is famous for its good roads, but where the pilgrim goes many of the paths are still bad. Everyone who travels with a definite goal in mind knows how unpleasant it is he must pass again over a part of the way that he thought was behind him. In Tosa the pilgrim is not spared this experience, for while at other temples he must go off the road several hundred meters, here he must walk for a whole hour to teach two of the temples, and at the 38th temple he must travel for seven hours. Of the 488 difficult ascents that the pilgrim enumerated in earlier times, a majority lie in Tosa. According to tradition, even Kōbō Daishi took pity on him and permitted him at one place to journey by boat for a considerable distance (at a place called *Gomen no Watashi*), "the most graciously-permitted passage by boat", between Usa and Nakanōchi) in order to spare him a most unpleasant section of the road, the eight ascents (*yasaka*). As a clowning weariness, even the miles are longer. If 48 *chō* made a *ri* in Awa, it now takes 50. Now is the time to strengthen the heart awakened to faith by all those obstacles, not allowing it to be deterred by difficulties and hindrances, giving it practice in the art of conduct and perseverance in the life of a pilgrim, even if such results cannot be brought about without shame and disgrace.

For this is the remarkable thing about it: not only the road and the landscape are different, but also the people and their attitude towards the pilgrims have changed. Just as the harbours of Tosa lie deeply intreached and hidden behind rocky walls, with small entrances that even sailors familiar with them can easily miss when surprised by a storm, so the character of the people of Tosa has also its hidden deeps and is not easily accessible. As the cliffs raise out of the sea defiant and gloomy, so the man of Tosa faces a stranger as if he were an enemy. The sun glitters more hotly over the sea, warmed by the Black Current from the south, and the blood runs more hotly in the veins of the man of Tosa and his eyes blaze daringly, nay, dangerously. The physical as well as the spiritual glance broadens with the immeasurable sea; hardihood is developed in the fight with the ocean – the courage toundertake responsibility, and, even more, the daring of the gambler – in quite a different manner than yonder on the Inland Sea, where there is always an island in sight in time of need. Once you leave this protecting harbour here, the saying runs: "*Ato de yoritsuku shima nashi*" (Henceforth there is no island to run to). Navigare ecesse est, vivere non est necesse: to the coral fisher, who day after day carries on his work at danger to his life, what does a human life matter? He lives turned away from the rest of Japan, and yet feels himself the best patriot of all. Strong in love and strong in hate, never looking behind and swift in decision, energetic and inspired by everything heroic – such do we find the inhabitants of Tosa to be. It is the country of great statesmen, but also that of murderers. The pilgrim still call it "Devil's Land" today and he did of old, and thinks with terror of the fact that there, scarcely 60 years ago, they killed all children after the second – a cruel two-child system to which the populace today still own their bodily fitness. "Devil's Land" says the pilgrim, and repeats the verse which he has already heard:

"Tosa wa onikuni   Yado ga nai"
(Tosa is the devil's land, No lodging there, we understand)

Shikoku-zaru wrote 26 years ago, "The people in Tosa are extremely indifferent to the Daishi, and the hosts and hostesses at the lodging as well as the ferrymen are all as greedy as they can be for money. It is like a pilgrimage into an enemy's country, I had previously been told. One finds but seldom the *to* mark on the hat of the pilgrims as a sign that they come from Tosa.

It appears that Buddhism is little suited to the character of the inhabitants of Tosa. Nowhere in Shikoku was Buddhism more cruelly persecuted after the Restoration than right here. It is a wonder that in spite of the ___ some very old buildings from the Kamakura era (Temples No. 24, 28, 32, 38) have survived those years of destructive fury. Some valuable treasures have been preserved too since the priests concealed them in good season (especially in Temples No. 34 and 31). Tosa is the only province in which, contrary to the spirit of the mountain-top Buddhism advocated by Kōbō Daishi, one temple of the pilgrimage was removed to a city after the Restoration in order to turn the original place of pilgrimage into a Shinto shrine pure and simple. As one result of that oppression, many temples in Tosa, even today, have fallen into decay through neglect – *sabishii*, as the Japanese say, and are just now beginning gradually to recover. But to this day the magnificent national treasures of Higashidera, which through Kōbō Daishi's presence at that temple as proved historically are doubly worthy of reverence (and also those of Godaisan near Kochi) are housed in a thoroughly unworthy way. Iwamotodera (No. 37), called in an earlier time the Five Temple, which had a splendid group of buildings with five great images of Buddha, saw its buildings and the temple lands plundered, and had to move to another place into a small branch temple, whose main hall with the roof pieced out with a piece of corrugated iron makes a pitiable impression.

How regardless the people of Tosa were of the pilgrimage at that time can be seen from the fact that for a long time no pilgrim might pass through Tosa, and there making the pilgrimage had to travel around Tosa from the 23rd temple on, where they offered sacrifices for the Tosa temples. Some time later resolution was passed in the provincial assembly in Kochi to admit only those pilgrims who could prove that they had in their possession all necessary means for their substance; and the money necessary to carry out such control was entered on the budget as "Cost of Driving Away the Pilgrims" (or Cost of Cleansing from Pilgrims". To be sure, the pilgrim of today can again journey unhindered through the countryside, but even yet he is not thought of very highly. In Tosa he who carries the pilgrim staff, even if he is in European clothing, as I was, is generally turned away from every decent inn, an experience which I myself had several times. "*Kappira*" or "*Tsukaete imasu*" ("Sorry" or "We are full") were the stereotypical answers. If one goes on a pilgrimage, they think in Tosa, he should take the consequences, and seek his lodging in the *kichinyado*, the "Wood Money Inns." And if one must undertake the pilgrimage in the summer, as I had to do, it may happen to him, as it did to me, that he is turned away even from these inns with the argument that they are too busy with raising silkworms. With an effort of soul one tears his glance away from richly-laden supper trays, which stand prepared for a feast under the mosquito net stretched out over the whole room, drags his tired limbs in the evening twilight over yet another high mountain, and down again into the valley, and must consider himself fortunate if he sits at length in the next temple, after long entreaty and refusal in the beginning, before a bowl of cold rice and two little slices of pickled radish; for a travelling companion who overtakes him the next day had to spend the same night under the open sky between shells and crabs on the seashore.

Is it chance that the scene of two legends in which Kūkai punishes hard-hearted people is laid in this very Tosa? That in the year 1901 Shikokuzaru experienced a great brawl at Tsudera in Tosa (No.25) between pilgrims and the priests of the temple, who tried to overcharge them? That at the same temple there was asked to me besides the accustomed fee an additional "10 sen for a brick for the bell-tower, which is to be rebuilt"? Really, the patience of the person on pilgrimage is many times put to a hard test even today on this section of the journey. Now in earlier times the devil's land angered the pilgrim even more, and could sour in him the milk of human kindness, one sees in the fact that, after Shikokuzaru, many pilgrims, when they had behind them the 39th temple, Terayama-ji near Sukumo, and had to experience once more in the beautiful little harbor town the humiliation of being able to get no shelter in any inn in the town itself. Even today the pilgrim lodgings lie upon the other side of the bridge in a suburb. When they climbed the Matsuozaka Pass, the boundary between Tosa and Iyo, and the entire bay of Sukumo with its countless islands, its bizarrely-shaped tongues of land, and many winding arms of the sea, lay before them: that then the pilgrims had no further glance for the unique panorama, but still keeping their backs turned on Tosa lifted up their garments and raised an evil-smelling memorial to the Devil's Land. This so-called Dung Monument of the Matsuozaka-Tōge (Pass) is no longer in existence, although even today the vegetation is very rank; but even to the present time the pilgrims breathe more freely when he has Tosa behind him.[61]

IYO

The houses of Sukumo, the city in Tosa, make a somewhat gloomy impression. In the first village that we came to in Iyo we found the woodwork of the houses, the door and a window frame, all painted a pleasant red and this was the case throughout the southern part of the province. The people too were agreeable and answered our greeting with something more than the one brief "Hai" such as we had heard in Tosa, a reply that discouraged all further conversations. A short time of listening to the people as they talked with one another was enough to bring to one's attention the difference between the short, clear and definite pronunciation of the people in Tosa and the kindly,

---

[61] Of course, I found in Tosa besides the less friendly folk some very amiable priests and other people. In the 27th temple, an obliging nun, who even asked me to write my name and so forth, in a special book; in Temples No.31 and 32, where a tea-kettle stood on the fire, with a written invitation to rest and take a cup of tea: the priest of the 33rd temple, and adherent of the Zen sect, who showed himself very agreeable and full of understanding. An elderly woman, placed in the home of acquaintances, who in 1926 led a blind 77-year-old woman around the 88 temples, told me that according to her experience one received alms plentifully even in Tosa, if one called on the people very early in the morning as long as the people are still in their sleeping garments, then one is sure to receive rice; after 10 o'clock in the morning, however, the shugyō (see p. 186) is fruitless.

100

almost drawling method of speech of those in Iyo. For example, nowhere have I heard the words *"arigatō gozai-masu"* (thank you) spoken with such a friendly note as just here; yes, even the one word *namoshi*[62], often used to round out sentences and employed almost everywhere, suffices to mark the kindly character of the people of Iyo. The larger part of the province is spread along the Japanese Inland Sea, that insuperably beautiful natural park. If one takes into consideration also the happy and yet meditative character of the inhabitants, it is no wonder that Iyo has been the land of the poets, especially of the writers of *haiku*. Where else are these pearls of Japanese poetry nourished in anything like the profusion that they here in the region which has given to Japan a Shiki, a Kyoshi, and a Hekigotō? To be sure, it is said that the inhabitants of Iyo are lacking in greatness. Nevertheless, the greatest Japanese dramatist, Chikamatsu Monzaemon, came on his mother's side from Iyo (Matsuyama), and especially in the north of the province, in Imabari[63], the people have never been lacking in a spirit of enterprise.

---

[62] This expletive answers in its significance to the expletive phrase used in many districts of Germany, "…sag ich Ihnen." (Translator's note: Or in English, "…I tell you" or "…, you know.")

[63] There was also a physician from Imabari who travelled in the 40s of the last century to Nagasaki, an order to learn vaccination from Siebold.

Therefore, the pilgrim rejoices when he comes to Iyo. Here, too, to be sure, he must conquer many high mountain passes, and must climb many steep peaks, even though he may not, as many do, add to this pilgrimage the ascent of the highest elevation on the island, Mount Ishizuchi. But he is walking at the same time upon the heights of faith. The temples are all well-placed; friendly priests exert themselves to the utmost in giving special instruction; there are temples where every pilgrim, be it ever so early in the day, is invited and urged to stay overnight, and where care is taken for his edification, as at Butsumoku-ji not far from Uwajima, at Koōn-ji near Komatsu, and at various others.[64]

If legend in Tosa knew enough to report the hard-hearted woman who denied potatoes or shellfish to the Daishi, or the demons who tried to annoy him at his devotions, it now tells about a friendly old man who lets him ride on his cow through the mountains, about a woman whom he helps in the pangs of childbirth, or about

---

[64] As a sign of the readiness of the people of Iyo to receive religion one can cite the fact that Christianity also found an entrance there very early. Among those who were converted in their time by Portuguese missionaries there were several samurai of the daimyō of Uwajima. In this city there are treasured even today in various houses little bronze (or brass) coins, which show on the obverse the portrait of Ignatius of Loyola, who stands with folded hands before the crucifix, and which are called by the people Kwannon-pennies (Kwannon sen) because of the Madonna pictured on the reverse.

Kwannon, who saves him from great danger at sea. Besides the places of pilgrimage there are also in Iyo an especially large number of traditions that have to do with the Daishi: here he carved an image of Buddha in a living tree; there he caused a spring to gust forth; somewhere else again in the 37th or the 42nd year of his life he performed the ceremony of the goma fire-mass, and carried out other rites, in order to exorcise the danger of that year. Most of the temples called *bangai*, standing outside of the prescribed succession, but nevertheless visited by a majority of the pilgrims, lie in Iyo. Among these are the splendid Shusseki-ji near Ōzu[65]; the Holy of Holies (*Okunoin*) of the 65th temple, Sankaku-ji; the wonderfully situated Senryū-ji, called from ancient times "the women's Kōya", which shelters all pilgrims and lets them share every evening in the ceremony of the goma fire-mass. "The people in Iyo are most kind-hearted. As one comes from hard and cold Tosa, he feels it with his first step. In the lodgings, the maid and

---

[65] There is a corner in the province of Iyo in which, remarkably enough, there are no temples of pilgrimage, although it has been proved that temples like Shusseki-ji, mentioned above, are very old and lay claim to connection with the Daishi. In a conversation on the subject, Professor Kageura gave the following explanation: At the beginning of the Tokugawa era there lived in Ōzu a very zealous priest of the Zen Sect named Bankei, through whose activity the Shingon sect, which had prevailed in that region for a long time, was almost wholly supplanted. This may have been at the very time when the number and the succession of the temples were fixed.

the mistress, on the street the chance passersby, all are extremely friendly," asserted Gyūho Itō, an author of haiku who lives in Tokyo, recently, after his return from the pilgrimage that he undertakes without fail once every year.[66]

SANUKI

Where the spirit of Daishi is so powerful among the populace the belief of the pilgrim is also greatly strengthened. The *shugyō* (religious practice in journeying) that he underwent in Tosa brings its fruits. Now he has attained to the rank of the Bodai, has become an awakened one and only a short time yet remains before he attains perfection and can enter into Nirvana.[67] The road to be travelled in Sanuki, 36 *ri* (140 kilometers; a *ri* in Iyo and Sanuki has only 36 *chō*), is scarely a ninth of the whole distance, disproportionately short. But here too there are many places rich in history and legend. To a certain extent we review once more the whole life of the Daishi, into whose home province we now enter.

At Iyandani-dera we tread with reverent awe the rock cave where he applied himself to religious practices

---

[66] Osaka Mainichi, at the beginning of December, 1927.
[67] One must always keep in mind with this explanation that it is meant in a figurative sense, but that according to the teaching of Kōbō Daishi the attainment of Buddhahood "in this body" is the goal of belief.

and left behind the picture of his parents as well as of himself. In Shusseki-ji we stand and look up at the face of the high precipice from which, according to legend, the six-year-old boy threw himself down, but was caught up by Shakamuni appearing in a cloud and brought back again to where he had been standing before. It is natural that Zentsū-ji should be especially memorable as the temple of Kūkai's birthplace, with Kotohira close at hand, where there is to be found the shrine of Kompira, the powerful guardian of all sea-farers, to whom even the Buddhist pilgrim does not neglect to show reverence. The road runs on to Yashima-ji, the witness of bloody battles; to Gokenzan, who five sharp peaks rise up like five swords fallen from Heaven; until finally we reach the 88th, Ōkubo-ji, hung around the crutches. When the pilgrim has this behind him, he can meet death in comfort: clad in the white garment that now bears the seals of all the holy places, he is certain to enter into Nirvana.

II. Situation of the Temples. Distribution according to sects. Chief Divinities

We could not find the road to the temples without sign-posts. Fortunately, pious folk have set up sign-posts everywhere at the numerous bends in the roads, many a time with the name of the donor and the information when and how often he has made the pilgrimage, many a time only a little field-stone with the swastika and a hand showing the direction to take. At important places, however, there is usually a four-sided stone about three feet high with information about the distances. Inscription and hand become weather-beaten very quickly in the Japanese climate, but they are always renewed without the need of anyone in authority troubling himself about the matter, as though someone or other friendly to pilgrims were travelling through the island with brush and paint pot instead of with staff and rosary. It is touching to discover, which one is at a certain spot on the way to the highest temple on the whole island, that there, where the path leads suddenly into the valley and the pilgrim unwillingly abandons some of the elevation that he has successfully attained, a pious woman has nailed to one arm of the ordinary sign-post a diamond-shaped board with the inscription: *"Kokoro kara ue wo henromichi ni arazu!"* (This information is from the heart. The upper road is not the pilgrim way.) Sign-posts are necessary until we come very close to a temple, for only seldom can we see from a distance the buildings and grounds as a whole. If the temple does not lies upon a high mountain, it lies hidden somewhere at the end of a valley, never in a city[68], and only seldom in a market-town (No.19)

---

[68] Temple No.30 in Kochi was designated as a place of pilgrimage only after the Restoration of 1867; up to that time, the 30th

or a village, as for example the first temple in Bandō known very well to many German prisoners of war.

In plan, the temples of the pilgrimage are not different from other temples. We find first the temple gate with two Deva kings, in front which hang countless straw sandals of all sizes as sacrificial gifts. Especially beautiful in its simple construction is the gate of Motoyama-ji (No.70), which dates from the Kamakura period and is under Imperial protection, while others such as those of Ishite-ji and Taisan-ji (No.51 and 52, both likewise under Imperial protection) are erected in the showy, almost overladen style of the Tokugawa period. Especially in Awa, but also in other places (Temple 65 and 87), we often find bell-tower and temple gate combined in one building. Where the temples lie on the plain, we see all the buildings united on one level after we have gone through the gate, so that we can overlook then at a glance; but on mountain sides or on peaks they are usually separated from one another by steep stone stairways, and there is often a good bit of climbing to be conquered after one has already entered the gate. Not far from the entrance there lies first the water basin (*chōzu-bashi*), usually a small stone trough covered with a roof, over which some little Japanese hand towels flutter in the wind, but sometimes a beautiful bronze basin

---

place of pilgrimage had laid two hours outside of Kochi. The Betsugū at Imabari, also, originally lay somewhere else.

in the form of a flower chalice, about which a water-spouting dragon twines itself. The basin of the Nagao-dera (No.87) is a strange sight, for it rests upon a recumbent cow and is shaded by a thick, three-cornered thatched roof.

The chief buildings are, however, the *Hondō* (Main Hall) and the *Daishi-dō* (Daishi Hall). In almost every case, the main hall is of one story. I saw it of two stories at only two temples (No. 15 and 78). In other respects, we find all possible styles of building that of the Shinto shrine not exception. The noble, flat style of the Kamakura period has been preserved in only a few cases. Such buildings are usually under Imperial protection. More abundant are the steeply sloping roofs of the Tokugawa period, seldom with an interruption reminiscent of our baroque style in the straight underline of the roof, which then is broadened to a kind of independent fore-roof. If we compare the various buildings, we can even trace out of the middle of the front slope of the roof, the growth of a gable, which finally reaches to the ridge-pole, as in the last temple of journey, Ōkubo-ji (see Picture Supplement. No. 37-44). In the main hall, the image of the chief divinity is set up, usually a statue, which in some cases was subsequently enclosed in another larges one. The 68th temple, however, has only a painted picture as the chief divinity. These images are usually hidden behind a curtain, and can be seen only on special festive occasions, when the ceremony of *kaichō* (Opening of the Curtain) takes place. Temple No. 64 is curious in that it possesses two Hondo, one for men and one for women).

The Daishi Hall is smaller, as rule. As the name implies, it is dedicated to the worship of Kōbō Daishi, corresponding therefore to the memorial chapel to the founder (*Kaisantō*) in other temples, and has a ground plan that is always strictly four-sided, while the roof in by far the larger number of temples runs up into a round knob. Most of the sacrificial- or thank-offerings of the pilgrims are dedicated to these buildings.

With regard to the next building, the bell-tower, two other forms can be distinguished, besides combination with the *Niōmon* (Gate of the Deva Kings) already mentioned. In the one, the bell hangs in the framework that is open on all sides; in the other, it is almost entirely out of sight, but butter guarded from the bad effects of weathering. The closed bell-towers are comparatively few; the 24th and the 51st temples afford two beautiful examples.

Some places of pilgrimage have also a Yakushi Hall, since for many pilgrims this healing divinity plays a great role. At some mountain temples, but also at the family temple of Kūkai, we find a kind of subterranean crypt, which serves as an Okunoin (Holy of Holies) for the temple. At the 45t and the 71st temples this is a rock-cave, which was probably used in very ancient times for ritualistic purposes.

Less than a fifth of the 88 places of pilgrimage boast of pagodas. Besides the one-storied one of Nagaodera (No.87) and the three-storied one of Kakurin-ji (No.20), we find five-storied ones at Motoyama-ji (No.70) and at Zentsū-ji (No.75), and even the treasure pagoda (hōtō), that can be recognized by the round middle part of the upper story, as shown by those at the 8th, the 19th and other temples. In spite of its lofty situation, Tairyū-ji (No.21) possesses a treasure pagoda as well as an ordinary pagoda of several stories. Here again, Ishite-ji (No.51) is the most interesting from the point of view of construction, with its three-storied pagoda that is under Imperial protection. As the temples that have no large pagodas, they are usually replaced by tiny replicas made of stone.

In Shikoku there is found still less frequently in the six-sided depository for sutras (kyōzō), which I could discover at only three temples (No.17, 20, 21)[69] whereas at others there is a beautiful gallery (No.67, 75) or a lovely storehouse for treasures (No.75).[70] On the whole, one must say that, apart from some exceptions, the splendor and the magnificence that distinguish the temples of Kyoto, Nara,

---

[69] Temple No.75 has a remarkable six or eight sided metal tower, which may serve also as a kyōzō.

[70] In regard to tsuyado and nōkyōsho, see later on p. 271 and p. 268.

and that region, are not to be found in the pilgrimage temples of the Daishi. The latter are more rural, simpler, but not on that account less charming, especially in their natural setting. To give only one or two examples: the gallery of Konotsuo-ji (No.67) with the bronze statue of the Jizō Bosatsu standing before it breathes a Greek beauty, which must delight every artistic eye, while the cemetery on the steep mountain slope at Onzan-ji (No.18), lighted up by the afternoon sun, is not surpassed in its peaceful mood even by the graves of the princes of Kōyasan.[71]

Distribution into Sects, Determination of the Chief Divinities

One might assume that all the temples belong to the Shingon sect, since the pilgrimage is traced back to the founder of this sect. Such, however, is not the case. Just as in the case of the pilgrimage to the 33 Kwannon temples, which belong to the three separate sects[72], there are also several sects represented among the Shikoku temples. Yet the Shingon temples, and among them those belonging to the older branch of Shingon, are so much more numerous that it is not outside the bounds of possibility that all the temples belonged at one time to this sect. Research on this point is lacking, and the greater parts of the ancient

---

[71] A complete list of the temples is given in the Supplement.
[72] Tendai 17, Shingon 13, Hossō 3.

documents have been destroyed by fire or in other catas-
trophes. Yet one could adduce in support of this view the
example of the 33rd temple, Sekkei-ji, which originally belonged to the Shingon sect under the name Shōrinzan Kō-
fuku-ji, then apparently suffered a decline, was restored
under the rule of Prince Chōsokabe Motochika, and raised
to the position of a votive- and burial-temple for him and
his family. At that time, the temple received the name
given first above, and was incorporated into the Zen sect,
to which it still belongs today.[73]

The present distribution according to sects is as
follows (it is significant that Nichiren-shū, Shin-shū, and
Jōdo-shū are not included, although many of their adherents make the pilgrimage):

Shingon	80	
Tendai	4	(No.45, 76, 82, 87)
Zen	3	(No.11, 15, 33)
Ji	1	(No.78)
The Shingon temples are subdivided into:		
Old Shingon	46	
New Shingon	25	
Shingon (Onoha, Tōjiha, Daigoha)	8	
Shingon Risshū	1	

---

[73] The hymns of the 26 temple, also, sound strongly the not of the
belief in Amida that belongs to the Jōdo sect or to the Shin sect.

The determination of the chief divinities shows a preponderance of the cults of Yakushi and of Kwannon. The chief divinities are:

Yakushi Nyorai at 23 temples
Kwannon Bosatsu at 28 temples
Amida Nyorai at 10 temples.
Dainichi Nyorai at 6 temples
Shaka Nyorai at 5 temples
Jizō Bosatsu at 5 temples
Fudō Myōō at 3 temples
Kokūzō Bosatsu at 3 temples
Miroku Bosatsu at 1 temple
Monju Bosatsu at 1 temple
Bishamonten at 1 temple
Batō Myōō at 1 temple
Daitsū Chishō Butsu at 1 temple

The central figure of Shingon, Dainichi Nyorai, therefore, stands out as chief divinity only six times, while on the other hand we find divinities, such as Daitsū Chishō Butsu, that play practically no part in Shingon, elevated to that high position. It is also remarkable that Batō Myōō, "The wonderful horse-headed king", should be the chief divinity of the 70th temple. It is a statue of Amida Nyorai with a horse's head, said to be the work of Kōbō Daishi, and under national protection.[74]

    That Kwannon and Yakushi far surpass the others in number indicates the age of the temples, for the cults of Kwannon and Yakushi were disseminated earliest in Japan, and were already at their height when Kōbō began his work.[75] Moreover, Japan shares with China and Tibet the broad distribution of the cult of Kwannon: the Dalai Lama is looked upon as an incarnation of Kwannon, while to the present day in China the worship of Kwannon can be said to be the heart of popular Buddhism. Every popular religion will always remain directed in large measure to matters of the present life. Kwannon, sitting upon her island in the southern sea and listening to all creatures who call upon her, is a figure in which an unusual power of attraction dwells, the more especially since she has been changed from a masculine divinity into a feminine one. In like manner, it is clear that Yakushi, the Healers, finds the way to the hearts of the people more quickly than Amida and Shaka, who require a much higher conception of the divine. This conception of religion, namely, concern with the things of this life, with immediate freedom from dis-

---

[74] It is common to find only Kwannon as the divinity adorned with a horse's head. Batō Tennō, the Horse-headed King of Heaven, is a subordinate divinity at the 12th temple.
[75] This can be recognized in the simple fact that among the statues under national protection as memorials those of Kwannon and Yakushi far outnumber all others.

ease and other needs, prevailed, however, however, not only among the people, but also at the court. Katō Tanaka in his research into the cult of Yakushi in Japan has taken the trouble to look through the old annals, and has found that almost always in the case of illness at the court pictures of Yakushi were donated, or the Yakushi sutra was read aloud or copied. The *Kokubun-ji* (national temples), also, that were erected in every province at the command of the Emperor Shōmu (724-749), were originally all dedicated to Yakushi; the great image of Buddha in Nara was designated as *Shōhonzon* (Chief Chief Divinity); while the temple of every province contains an image of Yakushi one *jō* six *shaku* (about five meters) high.[76] (Exceptions such as those in Echigo, Settsu, Sanuki, and Tosa go back to a later change). It is therefore not to be wondered at that more than a quarter of the Shikoku temple are Yakushi temples.

Upon closer analysis of the Kwannon temples, the interesting fact appears that almost all the temples of pilgrimage that can serve as chief representatives of mountain-top Buddhism are dedicated to either the 11-faced or the 1000-handed Kwannon. To the latter belong Unpen-ji (No66), Iyadana-ji (No.71), Negoro-ji (No.82), Yashima-ji (No.84), Ashizurizan (No.38), and Senryū-ji (No.58 Okunoin); and to the former Kōnomine-ji (No.27), Minodera (No.32), Suzōzan (No.44), Taisan-ji (No.52), and

---

[76] Editor: One jo = 3 meters; one shaku = 30cm

Sankaku-ji (No.65). To be sure, it is very doubtful whether these Kwannon temples were all founded by Gyōgi Bosatsu, to whom most of them trace their founding, but it is probable that we are concerned here with places of a religious cult arising before the time of Kōbō Daishi. Professor Tomita rightly asserts, therefore, that through his visits to these temples Kūkai received in his youth the first impulse to the mountain-top Buddhism later proclaimed by him. According to him, the 88 temples hold as important place, not only as places reminiscent of the Daishi in general, as well as the chief places of popular Buddhism, but also as places significant for the study of the historical development of the Daishi and his teaching. "That those busied with research about the Daishi look only to Kō-yasan in a discussion of mountain-top Buddhism and put aside the holy places of Shikoku with the remark that these arose first out of the belief in the future life, is indeed a serious mistake." Tomita considers it entirely possible, even probable, that after Kūkai' death some of his disciples withdrew to the mountain temples of Shikoku, in order to cultivate the master's teaching still further there. "It was a continual wonder to me in my earlier years of study of the history of the Shingon sect that mountain-top Buddhism was transformed immediately into city-Buddhism of the palace, and that after the Daishi, Rigen Daishi alone represented mountain-top Buddhism. In opposition to the mountain-top Buddhism of Abbot Shinnen on Kōyasan, there arose the city-Buddhism of the Shūei in Kyoto, and it was not long before the power of Kyoto so overcame Kō-yasan that nothing remained for Mukū and the other priests to do, but to give up Kōya. Whither would Mukū and the other priests inclined to mountain-top Buddhism have fled (if not to Shikoku)?"

III. Ryōbu Shintō at the 88 temples

It is a well-known fact that there belongs to the sects of Tendai and of Shingon that remarkable combination of Buddhism and Shintoism that goes by the name of Ryōbu Shintō, that is, two-fold Shintō. The teaching began in an age before Kūkai. Gyōgi Bosatsu was the first to proclaim it, and after him Ryōgen taught it. The core of their teaching, which was later developed further by priests of the Tendai sect, is expressed in the formula *honchisuijaku* (come down into this land). The Japanese divinities (*kami*) are incarnations of the Buddhas (*hotoke*); yet the latter first existed a priori, while the former first appeared a posteriori. This form of Ryōbu Shinto is also called Honjaku-Shinto from an abbreviation of the formula given above and contains in reality a slighting of kami in favour of the hotoke. It remained for the Daishi as to transform the teaching as to explain that the identity of the two consisted in formula *ryōbu-funi* (two-fold-not two), or *shinbutsu-dōtai* (kami-hotoke - one and the same form). The Shingon sect was predestined to such an amalgamation of the forms of belief, since the central figure of Shingon, Dainich Nyorai, the All-Illuminating, permits of almost complete identification with the great sun-goddess Amaterasu. The teaching gained ground, therefore, among high and low, especially in the Heian period, and it is not to be wondered at that we discover numerous traces of it at the Shikoku temples.

I need not enter into a discussion of the many little Shinto shrines that are to be found almost everywhere within the temple courtyards, since these are to be found in profusion elsewhere in Japan. It is more remarkable where we find a great *torii* at the entrance to a Buddhist temple, as in the case at Temples No.73, 79, 81 and others. At the two last named, the circumstances can be easily explained because of connections with the Emperor Sutoku, at the others the relation between the two lies in the fact that with the separation of Shinto and Buddhism at the beginning of the Meiji Era the buildings were indeed separated, but yet were left on the same piece of ground, so that within the temple courtyard one priest served at the Shinto shrine and another at the Buddhist temple. In many places, however, one feels as through the Shinto shrine were being gradually supplanted, as at Shōsan-ji (No.12). There, coming from the 11th temple, one walks to be sure through torii into the temple courtyard, where the Shinto shrine, despite the fact that it is managed by its own priest, looks very miserable beside the buildings of the pilgrimage temple.

It is still more remarkable that until the time of the Restoration that thirteen and even today nine of the 88 temples had and still have a purely Shinto name, or one reminiscent of Shinto.[77] Until the Meiji era there was in each of the four provinces a pilgrimage temple Ichi no Miya (or Ichinomiya-ji). Today in Awa and Sanuki we find a Shinto shrine, Ichi no Miya, close by the Buddhist temple. In Tosa after the Restoration all the property of the Ichi no Miya was taken away from the Buddhists and the place of pilgrimage was transferred to Anraku-ji in Kochi, while the Buddhist Ichi no Miya ni Iyo has been pulled down lately, because of the construction of a railroad in the neighbourhood, and set up again about one kilometer away from its former site. These Ichi no Miya are found as Shinto shrines in all parts of Japan. Their origin is explained in the following way (according to the Encyclo-

---

[77] No.13 Ichinomiya-ji (today- Dainchi-ji), No.27 Kōnomine-ji, No. 30 Ichinomiya (today – Anraku-ji), No.37 Kosha (today – Iwamoto-ji), No.41 Inarizan, No.47 and No.51 Kumanosan (compare p. 127), No.55 Betsugu, No57 Hachiman (today – Eifuku-ji), No.62 Ichinomiya, No64 Maegami-ji, No.68 Hachimangu, No.83 Ichinomiya.

paedia Japonies):

In the Nara period many shrines that could boast of an ancient origin received a kind of official status, that is, the governor of the province by order of the Emperor had to visit them once each year. Conditions of travel being what they were at the time, it was a visit consuming much time and money to all of the shrines became an impossibility, and therefore one shrine in the neighbourhood of the seat of government was decided upon as the chief one (*Shōsa*). Since it was, so to speak, the first shrine of the province, it was called Ichi no Miya. Usually only one shrine in each province was given such a preference, yet there were cases in which others in addition to the sōsha were designated, and were then called in order Ni no Miya, San no Miya, and so on. Sannomiya in Kobe may have come by its name in this way. It appears, however, that in the late Middle Ages in the time of the war disturbances (Ashikaga), when so many other things were overthrown, the traditions relating to the shrines were also wiped out. The Encyclopaedia Japanoica itself admits that among the places recognized officially today as Ichi no Miya there are many of very doubtful origins. Is it any wonder that we find in Iyo no less than three Ichinomiya? One is the 62 nd temple of the pilgrimage already mentioned; another is a Shinto shrine of small significance, situated, however, on the Soushagawa (the Chief Shrine River); the third, which is today officially recognized as the Ichinomiya, is O Mishima Jinja, lying on the island of Mishima, about thirty kilometers from Imabari in the Japanese Inland Sea. This shrine, called also Shikoku no Ichinomiya, looks back upon a very long past, and thanks to its situation on an island was saved from destruction during the war disturbance. There too Ryōbu Shinto flourished, for there were on Mishima no less than twenty-four Buddhist temples that originally were visited together as the 55th place of pilgrimage. Since, however, the Ichinomiya stood in a very close relation to the daimyō of Imabari, and, especially in times of danger from war, was appealed to for help as a protective divinity; since, on the other hand, a storm at the wrong time could prevent a passage across to the island to pray, sight of the 24 temples were moved at an early period to Imabari, but in the Tenshō era (1573-1592) they were all destroyed by fire. Finally, one of them, Nankōbō, was built again as a temple of pilgrimage, and through the patronage of the lords of Imabari gradually became prosperous again. At the time of the separation of Buddhism and Shintoism the chief statue was taken out of the Shinto shrine and placed in the Hall of Yakushi Nyorai, which served as the Main Hall from that time on. Here too Shinto shrines and Buddhist temple lie side by side. The place of pilgrimage, however, bears in addition to the name Nankōbō the designation Betsugū (Separate Shrine, Branch

Shrine). The mother-shrine of Betsugū, the Ichi no Miya of Omishima, as well as the Ichinomiya of Sanuki, trace their foundation back to Monmu Tennō (731-749) as its founder, which exact information is lacking in the case of the two others (No. 13 and 30).

In addition to the five above-mentioned temples of pilgrimage, we find an especially strong mixture of Shinto at the 27th temple in Tosa, Kōnomine-ji (Mountain for of the Gods Temple). According to tradition, Gyōgi founded this place by order of Emperor Shōmu (724-749), and worshipped there Izanagi, Izanami, and Amaterasu O Mikami. The chief Buddhist divinity is the 11-faced Kwannon, who is worshipped together with the Shinto divinities as *Sanjia Ichibutsu* (three kami – one hotoke). The Shinto shrine, however, lies on another slope, separated from the building of the pilgrimage temple.

At the 41st temple, Inarizan, we meet the God of Rice with his red foxes as the patron saint of the secret teaching.

> Kono kami wa
> Sankoku rufu no
> Mikkyo wo
> Mamorasetamō
> Chikai to zo kiku

I hear that this god (kami)

promises most graciously to

guard the secret teaching which is

spread abroad in the three lands

(India, China, Japan).

According to legend, for the sake of the spread of the Buddhistic teaching Kōbō Daishi on his journey around Shikoku came to an agreement here with Inari, and adored him as the supreme protecting divinity of Shikoku.[78] At this temple the buildings are so arranged that one walks under a great stone torii before he comes to the actual mountain. Upon the mountain lie the Hondō and Daishidō halfway up; between them there rises a second torii built of two stone pillars bound together with a straw rope wrapped in a sheet of copper, beyond which one ascends a flight of stone steps to the Shinto shrine situated on still higher ground. The dwellings of the two priests lie somewhat to the side, or below the other.

The war-god Hachiman, recurs in two temples as a Buddhist incarnation (No.57 and 68). The 57th temple is represented in the old guidebooks as Hachiman Iwashi-

---

[78] With this agreement with the Fox-god there accords very badly the legend that Kōbō banished foxes from Shikoku "until the time when iron brides should be built in Shikoku." Actually there are said to have been no foxes there until about 40 years ago.

mizu; today it is called Eifuku-ji, but its hymn (go eika) runs:

Kono yo ni wa
Yumi ya wo mamoru
Yawata nari
Mirai[79] wa hito wo
Sukū Midabutsu.

Arrow and bow protectest thou
in this world as Yawata (=Hachiman)
And in the future savest thou
All, all mankind, O Amida!

It seems that after the Restoration the pilgrimage temple was transferred from the Shinto shrine into a neighbouring Buddhist temple. The same thing happened at the 68th temple, which still bears the same name, remarkable for a Buddhist temple, of Hachiman-gū, but which is reality is no longer an independent temple. Since the early years of the Meiji era it has been combined with the 69th temple, Kwannon-ji where one makes the written offering at the same time for both places of pilgrimage. What is today called Hachiman-gū is really the Hall of

[79] Translator's note: In a guidebook of 40 years ago Raise with the same meaning is given instead of Mirai.

Yakushi Nyorai in Kwannon-ji, in which a hanging scroll picture of Amida Nyorai is worshipped as chief divnity. The old Hachiman-gū is now a Shinto shrine and lies on the peak of the same mountain.

That the divinity of Ishizuchi is adored as a Buddhistic incarnation at the 60th and the 64th temples we have already mentioned. The latter has the Shinto-ish sounding name of Maegami-ji (In Front God Temple), because the temple forms only an introductory stage to the Holy of Holies, the mountain peak, where the really god (*kami*) dwells. The 60th temple is the only one of the 88 that has preserved from the time of Ryōbu Shinto a Main Hall built in the pure style of a Shinto shrine.[80] After the separation of Buddhism and Shintoism this temple was abolished for a while, and entrusted the written offerings of the 60th place of pilgrimage to another temple, Seiraku-ji, lying at the foot of the same mountain. When Yokomine-ji was reinstated in its original rights, Seiraku-ji continued to give seals to the pilgrims, while it called itself Rokujūban Maefuda (Fore-ticket No.60; ticket here meaning temple, the place where the pilgrim gives up his ticket i.e. a pilgrimage temple). In the 59th temple I received, however, the following printed communication:

---

[80] At Kirihata-ji (No.10) also the Main Hall is reminiscent of Shinto construction, yet the building is of recent date, and the resemblance as I learned by questioning the priest there, is entirely a matter of chance.

"Please read this without fail."

"The next temple is Yokomine-ji, No.60. Among the 88 places that Kōbō Daishi[81] has been pleased to found in Shikoku, this Yokomine-ji is a holy mountain, the cause of special trouble and difficulties. More particularly, it is the temple of Mount Ishizuchi, where the revelation of the effigy of Ishizuchi Gongen is possible at any time. One may stay overnight in this temple, and, since a new bath has been built, gaze on the moon while bathing.

"At the foot of Yokomine-ji there are two so-called Maefuda, but since these are outside the succession, one loses a temple if he does not climb up to Yokomine-ji and there present his written offering. Do not, therefore, let yourself be led astray by them, but climb up with firm purpose, taking upon yourself trouble and difficulties, remembering the Daishi, who has founded these 88 temples: Reverence the chief divinity and complete the written sacrifice at the 60th temple!"

We spoke earlier of how little of the former glory remains at the 37th temple, Iwamoto-dera. Not always, however, did the populace put up with the abolition of temples so quietly. We are informed at the 81st temple that this was to have been transformed into a Shinto shrine after the Restoration because if was the burial place of the

---

[81] Before Kōbō there is a space left in the printing, as a mark of great respect.

Emperor Sutoku. The Buddhist priest, thinking only of his own advantage, furthered this plan in every imaginable way, but he had not reckoned on the fidelity of the people. They declared with one voice that with all the reverence for Emperor Sutoku the face remained that the pilgrimage temple of the Daishi was there first; they could not therefore allow the original holder of the place to be supplanted by the later comer. So the Buddhist temple alone was preserved. The soul of the Emperor was led in the first year of the Meiji Era (1868) to Sentsū-ji in Kyoto, and the administration of the building in which it had been reverenced up to that time was transferred in the 10th year of Meiji (1877) to the Kotohira Jinja. The matter, however, did not come an end there, but was taken to law, in the course of which this building and all the rest of the temple property were given back to the Buddhist temple, What trouble the Buddhists took in those years of persecution not to let the old buildings be handed over to destruction one can see in the fact that during these years the pagoda of the Sumiyoshi Jinja in Sakai near Osaka was pulled down, brought by sea to Shikoku, carried inland for 30 kilometers, and set up again at the 10th pilgrimage temple, were today it looks down from the mountain height into the valley of the Yoshino River.

Even there, where the separation of the two religions was as painful as it was at the 37th temple, Ryōbu

Shinto is still nurtured from the Buddhist side. At Iwa-moto-ji the five Shinto divinities of the old temple of pilgrimage, or rather, their appearance in Buddhist forms, are still worshipped today, and such is the case at other temples. Moreover, the reverse is seen in the worship as kami of Buddhist images in Shinto shrines. Horagashima Kunteki Jinja, lying near the present-day No.30 (Anraku-ji), received its name from a Buddhist priest named Kunteki, who has been connected with the old 30th temple, Ichino-miya.

Sometimes Ryōbu Shinto takes on the form of legend, as we have already seen above at Inarizan. Other examples at the 5th and the 8th temples, where Kūkai receives from Kumano Gongen, a divinity originally Shinto, in the one case a piece of consecrated wood, from which he carves a little statue; in the other case even a little golden image of Kwannon. At the 20th temple, according to legened, when Kūkai climbs up the mountain in order to worship (the god) Katsushima Myōjin, he finds a little golden statue of *Jizō* (like the two statues mentioned above, 1.8 inches high, which may point to a common origin for the legends), which is guarded by a pair of herons. This statue, now a national treasure, was especially worshipped, together with that of the 5th temple, by the Shōgun Minmoto Yoritomo, and is therefore called (like the one of the 5th temple) Shogun Jizō. It is too bad that at the present time sources and earlier works are still lacking from which the age of these various legends could be proved, the priority of the one or the other, and so forth. Yet they help to complete the picture that we have tried to sketch of the manifold connections between Buddhism and Shintoism at the 88 Shikoku temples.

C. The Pilgrim

I. His motive for making a pilgrimage

In a previous section the attempt was made to describe briefly the old explanation of the pilgrimage of the four provinces in the meaning of the four degrees of belief: Hosshin, Shugyō, Bodai and Nehan. We have, therefore, already explained the significance of the pilgrimage as a worthy religious practice. Many people undertake it only in this sense; just as every Japanese person strives once in his life to go to Ise, so it is the wish of many Buddhists, chiefly, however, the adherents of the Shingon sect, to make the Shikoku pilgrimage once. Besides, the custom, very wide-spread in the early days of the Tokugawa era, of the kaikoku, i.e., the journey to all famous places of Japanese culture, has not wholly died out, as I could see from several pilgrims' tickets (fuda, see p. 262).

Young people like to make the pilgrimage before marriage, since there is a saying that advises marriage after the Shikoku journey. This has especial weight in the province of Awa (Tokushima prefecture), and also in the northern part of Kyushu. Old people take the journey as a preparation for a blessed end of life. In many quarters of Japan, yes, even in the colonies as far off as Hawaii, there are associations that send someone every year to the 88 temples, being bound together by no other object than that of the one worthy practice.[82]

In many cases, however, the pilgrim seeks to attain sometimes definite through his journey, most frequently the healing of sickness, called *byōki-oroshi*. One of my students failed in his entrance examinations to the universities; as a consequence of excessive study and the excitement over his failure, he had a nervous breakdown and sat dejectedly at home, until the priest of the place sent him upon the pilgrimage, from which he returned healed and happy.

A young man suffers from cramps in the stomach, and the doctor is not able to help him. Finally, he goes on the pilgrimage and finds healing.

A young wife in Osaka is so injured in a difficult child-birth that she loses the use of her feet. As there seems to be no improvement after some months, her husband, a carpenter, builds a simple, two-wheeled card, a cripple's cart, as the Japanese call it, entrusts the new-born child to relatives, and betakes himself with his wife and his eight-year-old son to the pilgrimage. Deciding to visit the temple in reverse order, he begins at the 88th in Sanuki, and passes later through Iyō until he comes to the 52nd temple and from there to Dogo, the oldest hot-spring bath in Japan.

---

[82] According to Toyohiko Kagawa (Shisen wo koete, pub. 1920), Chapter 6), every village in the province of Awa sends (or sent) a man on the pilgrimage yearly.

In the evening he carries his wife on his back to the bath. Here it appears for the first time that she can move here feet again. Great rejoicing! The family prolongs its stay in the bath-resort, there is further improvement, but now their resources fail. The good inn-keeper, however, we are in Iyo, remember and not in Tosa, gives credit, yes, he even finds work for the carpenter, and when this is at an end, he borrows still more, until the wife, who meanwhile has learned to walk a little, is able to leave the cripple's cart (*izarikuruma*) behind her in the Ishite-ji temple at Dogo and to end the pilgrimage on foot. Such examples of healing of lame persons are relatively numerous; the foregoing example is only the latest to come to my ears (at the beginning of December, 1927). It would be a mistake to describe the healing here to the baths of Dogo alone, for those baths have only an insignificant power of healing – spiteful people even assert that they are best for healthy persons – and on the other hand there are enough cases where the cure took place quite apart from any course of treatment in mineral waters. At the same time that I was making the rounds, there was a man continuing his pilgrimage through Shikoku who at the 22nd temple had regained strength in his feet, after he had stayed for some days at the temple and had been instructed in the faith by the priest.[83]

---

[83] Witte cites another example of a miraculous healing at the 51st temple in "Japan zwischen zwei Kulturen" (Japan Between Two

The young man with stomach trouble was only one of several persons who had been healed with whom I came in contact. It is quite clear that the changed manner of living; the constant outdoor life, fanned now by the fresh, clear mountain wind, now by the strengthening, salt sea-breeze; the freedom from all domestic care; the common journey with congenial people filled with the same purpose; all create a favorable atmosphere for a cure. Numerous priests with whom I have spoken about this matter have frankly admitted as much to me. They emphasized also, however, and not, it seemed to me, unduly – the fact that the natural method of healing (*shizen ryōhō*), as they called it, was not enough by itself, but that to a considerable degree faith also contributed towards the cure, even though it might be only through effecting in the ill person a change of attitude towards his suffering. Every year in Shikoku, as in Lourdes and other places of pilgrimage in Europe, cures that border on the miraculous take place; and it would be as fruitless to try to persuade the person freed on Shikoku of his suffering that he did not owe his cure to the mercy (*go riyaku*) of the Daishi, as to try to take away the belief in the grace and miraculous power of the Virgin Mary from the person healed in Lourdes.

When they have received their health again, numerous pilgrims make another journey around Shikoku (*on reimawari*, the round of gratitude), and join the great number of those who make the pilgrimage in fulfillment of some vow or other, or in thankfulness for deliverance from illness, from distress at sea, or from danger in war. Here is one example (for another, see later p. 234). Mr. T. Miyauchi, the son of a sake brewer, is in Tokyo at the time of the great earthquake of September 1, 1923. His aunt in Nagoya has a vision two days before the catastrophe and telegraphs to the family a warning, which is however not taken seriously. Mr. Miyauchi is one of those who are in the courtyard of the military cloth factory; 37,000 people are burned alive there, and only two hundred, he among them, are dragged out, unconscious but still living, from the mass of half-charred victims. He aunt ascribes the rescue to the prayers which she had incessantly sent up to Heaven for him on that day, and determines that he, who still half doubting is already half inclined to belief, shall make a pilgrimage in thankfulness. In Iyo, at Kōon-ji, the abbot completes his conversion.

Mrs. Ei Arai, eighty-five years old, from Okayama prefecture, has carried on an uninterrupted pilgrimage of thankfulness since she was sixty-one, because her granddaughter was cured of deafness and became a happy bride; after each round she returns for a short time to her home, in order to provide herself again with what she needs. Numberless other examples could be given. The pilgrim who makes the pilgrimage does not do it always for his own sake; it is not rare to find him visiting the temples for someone else. Such a vicarious journey is called *go daisen*, and here belong also the instances cited above, where a community sends one or several representatives annually to Shikoku. It is the same in performance even though somewhat different in meaning, when the journey is undertaken for the spiritual welfare of deceased relatives. We frequently find such persons, chiefly sons and daughters, who want in this way to render to their parents after death one more service of filial love; it even happens that they carry with them the ashes of the ancestral tablet of the deceased person.

One more motive may be mentioned, among those that urge on many people along the highways of Shikoku. Sometimes there comes moments in our lives when simply everything fails; when every undertaking, every plan, no matter how well thought out, miscarries; when what we had counted on as most secure is overturned; a farmer's harvest fails; his ox is carried off by disease; thieves have broken in and stolen the best of what little is left; and in addition to all this misfortune the young married daughter is sent home by the family of the bridegroom for what seems no reason at all, making them the laughing-stock of the neighbors and acquaintances, and bringing discord into the house, where everyone wants to charge someone else with the guilt of the unsuccessful union. In such cases many Japanese reach for poison, throw themselves onto the railroad track in front of a train locomotive, or cast themselves into the sea. Others however tie up their bundles, equip themselves as well or as poorly as their means allow, and set off on a pilgrimage. And to them also there is brought the longed-for help through escape from the confines of their daily live, which has almost crushed them, through the change in their mode of life, through the distance gained away from what made them miserable, and most important of all through faith, which is confirmed in the course of the journey. Even if luck has not changed for them on their return, they are able to see life from another angle, and this often makes possible a change of fate and sets them on the right road.

By far the largest number of pilgrims undertakes the pilgrimage from one or from several of the reasons given above. It we make a comparison with pilgrimage customs in Roman Catholic countries, there are innumerable parallels to be drawn. The opinion – held for the most part by those who have never held the pilgrim staff in their hands – that a great number of people undertake the Shikoku journey more for recreation or for pleasure, I have found by experience to be false. It is true that in the Tokugawa era there came into the custom of pilgrimage, especially of that to the thirty-three temple of Kwannon, a theatrical, fashionable element through the influence of drama such as Awa no Jūrōbei.⁸⁴ On some shorter pilgrimages, e.g., on that around the island of Awaji, there may be those who count upon enjoying it, like Kaname's father-in-law in Tanizaki Junichiro's newest novel, Tade kū Mushi, but according to what I have seen in Shikoku, this pilgrimage is even for a Japanese person not an unmixed pleasure!

Like everyone else, he understands the demand made upon him to live on poor fare and expose his body for weeks at a time to the attacks of vermin in ramshackle shelters. He may keep on with the journey for a while, but if it is undertaken only for pleasure and without a loftier purpose, the pilgrim will soon lose the desire to continue. Even I had my critical hours, in which I was closer to turning around then to continuing, and from all that I have seen and heard, I believe that the "pleasure-travellers" on

---

⁸⁴ Awa no Jurobei is a drama based on an historical event: Jūrōbei becomes a rōnin for some reason or other – drama and history diverge at this point, there former extenuating the mater – and travels as a robber with his wife, O Yumi, through the countryside; the grandfather sends the young child, called O Tsuru, well supplied with funds, upon the pilgrimage to the thirty-three Kwannon temples; on the way the child is attacked suddenly by the father, and since she refuses to hand over the money, is killed by her own father.
The somewhat theatrical costume of the child appears to have influenced pilgrim fashions, for instead of the simple white costume worn up to that time colored garments, especially some edged with red, were worn. But I found no yielding to such customs in Shikoku.

the Shikoku round are soon disillusioned and are therefore few and far between. On the other hand, there is a class of "professional travelers", whose livelihood is based on the pilgrimage, and with whom we shall have to deal later.

II. His Equipment

In the equipment of the pilgrim we see the same conservative tendency that lends its character to the whole pilgrimage. There have been very few changes since Daishi roamed over the wilderness of Shikoku, performing his devotion and saying his prayers at the mountain temples, and these changes are entirely dependent on the change in cultural condition; for it is clear that, in the era of cotton, preference will be given on financial grounds to the cotton garment rather than to that of pure linen, just as the tabi with rubber soles are now in the process of supplanting the ordinary tabi and the straw soles. Furthermore, it is to be expected that there are many variations on the equipment as described above, since the pilgrims come from all regions of Japan, many of the probably with another pilgrimage behind them, and since there is no control over such matters. It would never occur to anyone to call a pilgrim to account because something about his equipment was not quite regular; e.g., many today who cannot afford the white costume go in dark clothing, but it is no obstacle to saying that the equipment as we describe it here is des-ignated as correct and universally authentic. The various pilgrim costumes of the other pilgrim-ways and their influence on each other would be a worthy study, but one probably difficult to carry out. On Shikoku alone there are two distinct types besides the pilgrims to the eighty-eight temples: a) the Ishizuchi pilgrims, recognizable chiefly by their staffs and conch-shell horns, which are nowadays only a curiosity, but which were necessary in the old times in the wilderness of the mountains for signaling for help in case of losing the way, or in a fog[85], and b) those making the ascent of Tsurugi, the second highest mountain in Shikoku.

In the olden times the following articles belonged to the pilgrim costume:

A simple linen garment (*asa no kimono*)

A broad hat woven of fine bamboo strips

A straw sack in which were carried the articles needed for the journey (*nidawara*)

A bag hung around the neck (like the begging pouch of our mendicant monks) to receive gifts (*sanya or san-e no fukuro*) or a box (*mentsū*)

---

[85] Here is probably one of the few places where the result of Shugendo is to be seen at the present day in Shikoku. A charm of the 60th temple, at which the divinity of Mount Ishizuchi is worshipped, displays such a conch-shell with an appropriate inscription.

Ashinaka zōri, i.e., zōri which extended only over the sole of the foot, but did not cover the heel.

Pilgrim staff, called *kongōzue* (diamond staff)

Rosary *(juzu)*

Ticket-clamps *(fudabasami)*

Leggings *(kyahan)*

In contrast to the above, the equipment of the present day consists of the following:

A simple garment of white cotton cloth

A broad hat made of rushes *(sugegasa)*

A woven basket with a portable frame *(nigōri or nidai)* for carrying needed articles.

A pouch hanging at the side from the shoulder, for gifts *(zudabukuro)*; only the priests now carry the san-e bukuro.

Straw sandals which cover soles and heels *(waraji)*, and in recent times tabi with rubber soles

Pilgrim staff, rosary, ticket-clamps or more often ticket-box, leggings, hand-protectors *(tekkō)*, seat-apron *(shirizuke)*.

It is hard to determine when the last three-named articles of the costume came into use. The book, *Shikokudō Shi-nan,* says in the preface: "Straw sack for baggage, eating-box *(mentsū)*, hat, staff, leggings, *ashinaka,* and the rest of the equipment are left to the judgment of the individual; it would be better to go in ashinaka; for straw sandals make the hands dirty (in putting them on and taking them off) and at many temples there is no water for washing."[86]

---

[86] With these statements may be compared the equipment of the yamabushi of that time, which was exactly prescribed, and in which every object had it definite place and referred in some way or other to the teaching of the jishin sokubutsu, which corresponds to the sokushin jōbutsu of Shingon (see. p. 57). There are a twelve-part and a sixteen-part equipment, but the latter consists of the former with four additional articles. The names of the various articles are as follows:

1. suzukake – black outer garment (shawl)
2. yuikesa – the kasaya, not hanging at the side, but folded and laid around the neck, and therefore yui=neckband-kasaya.
3. tokin – small cap, like the caps with visors of some student clubs in Germany. The character is read ordinarily zukin.
4. hōra – great conch-shell, ordinarily called hora.
5. irataka-nenju – rosary, whose beads have many corners.
6. shakujō – staff with rings for beating time when reciting the sutras.
7. hangai – small standard with canopy
8. oizure – portable shrine, a frame with a box in which there is an image of Buddha.
9. katabako – shoulder-box, probably a box carried over the shoulder.
10. kongōjō – pilgrim staff
11. hikishiki – seat-apron, made of deer hide or bearskin
12. gyahan – leggings, ordinarily called kyahan.
13. hi-ōgi – a kind of fan made of thuya-wood
14. shibachi – a brush knife
15. sōjō (hashira nawa) – rope (for lassoing evil spirits)

All the woodcuts in the same book, however, show the pilgrim in dark leggings, but without hand-protectors and without seat-aprons. *Shikoku Henreidō Shi-nan Sōho Daisei*, a book of the Bunkwa era, prints the preface of the older book word for word, but has only one illustration of three pilgrims, of which two, a man and a woman, wear black leggings, and the third white leggings, dark hand-protectors, and even a seat-apron. Because of their form, there can scarcely be a question that hand-protectors and leggings, and apparently also the seat-apron, have been taken over from the armor of the middle ages. A certain antiquity in these articles of equipment is proved also by the fact that in regions where Shingon and Tendai prevail a dead person is usually laid in the casket at the time of burial wearing hand-protectors and leggings.

The Garment

As has already been stated, the garment is made of simple white cloth in the usual cut of the Japanese kimono under it is worn an undergarment (*juban*) of the same material. Most of the pilgrims have stamped upon the garment at each temple the red stamp with the name of the temple and the seal of the chief divinity, and perhaps also at one or two especially famous places the pictures of the

---

16. waraji – straw sandals.

142

chief divinities. This garment with the stamps is very ari-gatai[87], the pilgrim preserves it for the rest of his life, and has himself clothed in it at the hour of his death. The protection and intercession of all the divinities of the eighty-eight temples assure him a blessed end. On this account, many pilgrims, in order not to smudge their shroud, take with them another kimono wrapped in a white cloth; this they unpack carefully at each temple, and pack it away again just as carefully after it has been stamped.

The Hat

In the illustration of the Jōkyō era almost all hats have the form of an obtuse cone, exactly corresponding therefore to the form of the ancient knightly hat (*chingasa*); only two show the form of a flattened dome, which might be by chance. In the picture from the Bunkwa era, every one of the three pilgrims hats is different. One is cone-shaped, another shows in cross-section the form of a parabola, and the third, that of a segment of a sphere with rounded edges. Even today one finds various shapes, but from my experience the rule is the spherical segment with

---

[87] For the religious significance of this word, that today has been reduced to a formal expression of thanks in everyday use, see Gundert, "Der Shintoisms im Japanischen Noh-Drama", Mitt.d.D.Ges.f.Nat.und Volkerk, Ostasiens, Bd. XIX, p.227.

rounded edges or the flattened dome. The hat has a diameter of 60 centimeters and a depth of 15 to 20 centimeters. In the middle there is a frame fitted to the shape of the head, in order that the hat may not rest directly upon the head. From the middle of the inner flat surface of the hat there hang down over the frame just described loops made of cloth string lined with wadding, which are pulled together by a white band under the chin, to keep the hat in place. If there were only a simple band, the hat would be too easily pushed out of place. On the outer surface of the hat, the guide-book prescribes the following verses to be written outward from the middle in suitable divisions in the shape of rays:

> Out of error, the three worlds
> Out of awakening, the ten thousand heavens.

> In the beginning was neither East nor West
> Where was then North, where was then South?

Name and origin of the pilgrim are also to be seen on the hat. The people of Shikoku can be recognized by the fact that they wear in a circle the character i for Iyo, to for Tosa, sa for Sanuki and a for Awa. The *to*, however, is seen relatively rarely.

The Portable Shrine

In old pictures, e.g., in illustrations for novels, which show pilgrims on the Saikoku pilgrim way, we find the oizure, a frame which covers the back for its entire length, and to the upper end of which is fastened the pilgrim hat, which consequently soars, or more properly rocks, over the head of the pilgrim. In the lower part of the frame there is likely to be a shrine with an image of Buddha. The reproductions of the Shikoku pilgrims of the Genroku era and later show, however, only a simple, oblong bundle, called oidawara or nidawara; the ends of the bands with which this bundle, really a rice-sack, was tied on at both sides, are tied together at the front of the neck, as we sometimes see laundrymen or pedlars carrying their bundles of laundry or wares even today. The pilgrim nowadays generally has a woven basket, a miniature of the corded travel-baskets (*kōri*) so popular in Japan, which is about ten centimeters long, 25 centimeters wide, and when empty about the same in height. This little basket rests upon a wooden support, from which the straps supporting the frame go out. These hold the little basket firmly on the frame and are held together by bands at two places on the breast.

In addition to washable clothing (sleeping garment, *nemaki*; dressing-robe, *yukata*; etc), the pack contains the waterproof (*amagu*), i.e., usually only a large piece of oiled paper or a kind of circular cape with or without hood of the same material, a primitive protection against downpours of rain, but one that is not ineffectual, as I can testify from experience, if these downpours are not too heavy. The pilgrim of long agoused instead a piece of rush matting, goza, such as the pilgrims to Mount Fuji, Mount Asama, and also in Shikoku to Mount Tsurugi, use even today. There is also in the pack a small basket in the form of a bentō-box, for gifts of food and other necessities received along the way. On a pilgrimage for a deceased person, this basket often contains the ashes or the ancestral tablet of the departed.

Mentsū and Zudabukuro

The knapsack hanging from the neck, called mentsū or ebako is worn mostly by the flute-playing priests (*komusō*), who go around collecting gifts with their whole faces concealed by bell-shaped hats, and is used on the pilgrimage in Shikoku today only by priests. The guidebook of the Jōkyō era, that of the Bunkwa era, and later that of the Tempo era mention, however, only this word in connection with the equipment. Ordinary people nowadays carry instead a kind of pouch of white cloth on the left side. This pouch is suspended on a wide band leading over the right shoulder. In his pouch the pilgrim keeps his pilgrim book and his guidebook; it serves him also as a place to put the gifts that are handed to him. This pouch is called *zudabukuro*.

Footwear

As we saw above, it is advised in the introduction to *Shikokudō Shi-nan* to use *ashinaka zōri*, i.e., zōri which do not cover the whole underside of the foot, but afford protection only to the real sole. Complete zōri would have been especially troublesome in mountain climbing, which those straw sandals called in the old books *warouzu* and today usually waraji proved to be unpractical, because they could not be taken off without the aid of the hands, which often could not be washed when they were soiled, because of the lack of water. Today there is provision made at every temple for water, and therefore we see now another change in progress, as more people every year are exchanging the straw sandals for the "thousand-mile-stockings" (*senritabi*), as the tabi with rubber soles are generally called. The pilgrim law printed later (p. 167) still recommends the straw sandals, ostensibly on grounds of practicality, since on steep paths it is easy to slip in the thousand-mile-stockings But according to pilgrims whom I questioned about the matter, the rubber tabi are far more practical; one can walk more firmly than in waraji, and can get along with one pair for the entire journey, while with straw sandals one needs a new pair every two or three days, and often two pairs a day go to pieces on rough mountain paths. As yet, neither our European footgear not our European dress have come into general use of the pilgrimage.

The Staff

One of the most important articles of equipment is the pilgrim staff. It is, to wit, nothing more and nothing less than the representative of the Daishi; therefore, the pilgrim law prescribes that we handle it "beautifully and gently" (*go teinei ni*), and when we arrive at a shelter in the evening, we should clean off the dirt on it before we wash our own feet. In the shelter we give it the place of honor, that it, we place it in the niche (*tokonoma*) and have a short devotional service, before we make ourselves comfortable in the room. Many people even make a cover of white cloth about eight inches long to put over the upper end of this staff, in order to protect it, and so that the Sanskrit characters to be found there may not become soiled through the dirt and sweat of the hands. If one comes across a bit of water during the day, it is good to wash the point of the staff in it; then one's feet will become strong and not sore. If it should happen that there is no signpost at a crossroad, the stick becomes an oracle; one stands it upright and then lets it go, and it points out the proper path.[88]

There are various kinds of pilgrim staffs: the smooth, round staff of Japanese cypress (*hinokizue*); the tall, staff furnished with rings (*shakujō*); and others. The staff prescribed for the Shikoku pilgrimage is a simple, light stick of cedar wood; it is four-sided; each side represents one of the stages of belief described above (p. 90). Lower down, however, the edges are leveled off, so that the stick becomes eight-sided (or even round) in its lowest part, so that the stick falls into five divisions, one long and four shorter. With such divisions it becomes a facsimile of the stupa, although the forms (cube, ball, pyramid, hemisphere, conic ball) are not imitated[89], and represents the five elements. The lowest division, which is also the longest, is the earth, the others symbolizing water, fire, air, and ether, and the primary colors corresponding to the five elements, yellow, white, red, black (dark), and blue. Upon the sides of the stick there are inscribed in India ink the following verses in Sanskrit characters, one verse to a side:

---

[88] The pilgrim if firmly convinced that this oracle is, as a rule, right. On the first day of my journey there accompanied me a young Buddhist who turned to the oracle in one place and used it with success. At another crossroad-we had turned aside from the real pilgrim road because of the rain in order to reach the highway – our own judgment carried us astray.

[89] And yet, I have seen the stick of a Saikoku pilgrim on which the forms of the "stupa" were exactly imitated.

1st side – a ba ra ba kya

2nd side – aa baa raa baa kyaa

3rd side – an ban ran ban kyan

4th side – ak bak rak bak kyak

Under the characters on the first side there is written:

"Junpai shitatematsuru Shikoku hachijūhakkasho dōgyō futari"

Pilgrimage to the eighty-eight places in Shikoku performed reverently by two travelling companions

and upon the third side are written the name and the origin of the pilgrim.

The stick is called kongozue.[90] Since Kōbō Daishi is the reincarnation of Dainichi Nyorai, who name as ruler of the world of unchangeable ideas – the kongōkai -, kongō, means "diamond", and was passed down to Kōbō Daishi also; since moreover the stick, as we saw, is a facsimile of

---

[90] Bukkyō Daijiten not only gives a variant reading, but mentions the pilgrim staff only secondarily. It next describes an article of worship of the same name, whose four sides, however, are about 1.5 inches wide, and whose whole circumference of 6 inches has the significance of the six Mahaabhūta's, the six great elements of earth, water, fire, air, ether, and consciousness.

the "stupa" or gorintō, representing the five elements of the kongōkai, and serves as proxy for the Daishi, who is making the pilgrimage with us; there should be little doubt as to the origin and the significance of the staff. Some, however, such as Bukkyō Daijiten and the dictionary Kotoba no Izumi (Gensen), go back for the meaning of the stick to the *tokko* (less correct, dokko), the prong (spear), that is, to the lightning flash that Indra holds in his hand for the conquest of evil spirits.

Indeed, tokko, sanko and goko (one-pronged spear, trident and five-pronged spear) play a great role in Shingon. In Shikoku two also identical legends run parallel to the legend of the founding of Koyasan, according to which Kūkai, before his return from China, threw the sanko into the air on the shore, and later found it hanging on the branch of a fir tree on the top of Mount Kōya. In one of these legends it is said that the tokko which he threw into the air landed in a tree in the place where today the 36th temple stands; in the other, that the five temples that until the Meiji Era composed No.37 of the places of pilgrimages arose on the place where fell the five-pronged spear that he hurled into the air.

The staff is carried in the right hand, while the rosary is twined around the left.

Tickets and the Ticket-clamp

Like the Saikoku pilgrim, the one on Shikoku also leaves behind him at every temple he visits a ticket, called a *fuda*, which we might call his visiting card, if the modern expression did not awaken false conceptions. I shall therefore use the simple word "ticket." The Japanese expression for the giving up of the tickets is *fuda wo utsu*, i.e., posting up the ticket. The word *utsu* (to hit) is even used in pilgrim speech directly for "to visit" or "to perform (one's task)", for example, "*Gojūban wo moūchimashita ka?*" (Have you already visited No.50?), or "*Watakushi wa bangai wo uchimasen.*" (I am not visiting the special temples which lie outside of the regular round.) The word takes on meaning when we remember that the oldest surviving ticket, the one at the sacred shrine of Enmyō-ji (No. 53), is made of sheet copper and is actually posted up; and that the fuda, as the Chinese character shows, was originally used chiefly to denote a small wooden board; and that even today wooden fuda, quite apart from the *tatefuda*, are used in many ways in theatres, warehouses, banks, and so forth. Since a gift to each temple was originally connected with the pilgrimage (see the Written Offering. p. 268), and since in many temples even to the present day the names of the givers are written on small boards and nailed to a frame, I believe that I may venture the opinion that utsu, the fastening up of the fuda, is the oldest usage, even if only the exceptional pilgrim or group of pilgrims nails up such wooden or copper tickets at the present time.[91] To be sure, this opinion stands in opposition to the legend that explains the origin of the posting up of tickets, which we repeat in full in the following paragraphs, since it brings out the justification of the pilgrimage taken in reverse order, and shows besides how various temples and places lying far apart are bound together through legend.

The Tale of Saburō Emon

In the village of Ebara not far from Matsuyama there lived a rich, but hard-hearted man, called Saburō Emon, who called his own eight blooming children. When Kūkai journeyed through Shikoku, he stopped for some time in this region, and undertook to bring this man to a better view of life. He came therefore to the gate of the rich man many days in succession, said his prayers, and stretched out his iron bowl for gifts. Emon sent him away every time, but as Kūkai always came back again, he finally became angry, took a stick, and with knocked the bowl from the hand of the priest. It fell to the ground and broke in eight pieces. On the same day Emon's children, one after another, became sick and died, to the great sor-

---

[91] Several of such tickets are to be found at every temple, although they are not always of plain wood, but also of black lacquer with red or gold lettering, and so forth.

row of their parents. Even to the present day, eight knolls[92] rising from the dust that Kūkai threw upon the wind from a distance are designated as the eight graves, and the Eight-Knoll-Temple (Yasaka-ji) is the 47th of the temples of the pilgrimage. Saburō Emon repented of his hard-heartedness and his anger towards the priest, whose holiness he now recognized for the first time, and he set out for the little temple that had served the priest as a stopping place, to ask for forgiveness. But when he arrived there, the one he sought for had already gone on. Emon therefore took a sheet of paper, folded it three times, and wrote his name on one of the six tickets he obtained in this way. He pasted this ticket up in the temple and went on after Kūkai, but to whatever place he came, the saint had already gone on before. Emon left a ticket behind him every time and followed the road by which the other had gone. Twenty times he thus covered the road around Shikoku, his troubles and exertion had made him old and weak, and yet he had not overtaken Kūkai. Then he decided to make a last attempt; he travelled in the opposite direction, and at last, near to death, he met him for whom he had long sought between the 13th and the 12th temples. The priest willingly conferred upon him absolution, and granted his request that he might be born once more into

---

[92] Even today one can see these mounds, which are described by archeologists as prehistoric graves.

this world, in order to atone for his former failure.

In July of the following year there was born in the house of the ruler of Iyo, Yasukata Ochi Kōno, a son, whose left hand was convulsively closed from birth. It did not open until a festival day during his third year, when there fell from it to the earth a stone on which, by looking closely, one could distinguish faintly the characters "Saburō Emon."[93] This stone Emon had received before his death from Kūkai, as a sign of the promise made to him. The son of the prince was therefore the reincarnation of Saburō Emon. After he had become ruler of Iyo, he had the 51st temple, which up to that time had been called Anyō-ji, rebuilt in a magnificent way, and presented the temple with the stone, which today is still preserved there – it is even a national treasure. Since then, that place of pilgrimage has been called Ishite-ji (Stone-hand Temple), but in the song of the temple the old name persists.

At the place where, according to the legend, Emon left his first ticket, a priest who made the Shikoku pilgrimage about five years ago "received from the Daishi in a dream the instruction to erect a temple." At present, it is only a rather modest little hall, in which are set up two

---

[93] The same moment appears in the history of Tachibana no Yoshine, whose son became the founder of the 27th Kwannon temple, the Shoshasan; only instead of a stone a needle was involved.

statues, one of the Daish and one of Saburō Emon, made of the tickets of pilgrims, while on the wall several badly painted hanging scroll pictures graphically tell the above story. The legend itself is very old and is reported in the earliest guidebooks.[94] As one can perceive from the tale, the pilgrim's ticket should consist of the sixth part of a piece of Japanese hanshi, which is about 13.5 inches wide and 10 inches long. The ticket would therefore be 2 1/4 inches wide and 10 inches long. I have actually found tickets of this size when the pilgrims themselves had written the whole ticket. The people nowadays who do this are usually older folks or women from the country. The majority, on the contrary, use the tickets already printed, which are obtainable everywhere, and on which one has only to write name and dwelling, provided that one has not these also printed. Since the paper of the printed tickets is of a quality much inferior to the hanshi, this transition to mechanization and popularization is not

---

[94] Through the kindness of Professor Kageura, I had access to a copy of a very old chronicle, *Futanashū* (Collection of Futana, Futana being the ancient name for Iyo), dated in the Jōkyō era, in which this legend was already metioned, and so was able to correct the version current today. The origin of the tickets at the 33 temples of Saikoku goes back to the fact that the Emperor Kwasan wrote a poem to Kwannon of Kogawa upon a ticket. This fuda, preserved to this day, dates however from the 16th Century, and is therefore 570 to 580 years younger than the Emperor Kwasan, and not older than the earliest ticket of the Shikoku temples (see Inamura, p.594)

to be welcomed. Most of the printed tickets are of dimensions smaller than those mentioned above, and frequently have in addition to the inscription a small representation of the so-called Kōya Daishi.[95] The guidebook, however, expresses itself in strong words against such a sacrilege: "Many people make the pilgrimage with tickets that quite improperly show on the upper end the sublime image of the Daishi; if through want of foresight such a ticket falls upon the street, it becomes liable to untold desecration: to being trampled upon by dirty feet, to being covered with cow or horse manure, and the like. Where is the piety of such people? There is a lack of harmony between their words and their deeds."

The customary ticket of the Shikoku pilgrim is therefore a simple, long, white rectangle. The point at the upper end, as the ticket of the pilgrimage to the 33 temples of Kwannon pictured in the Encyclopaedia Japonica shows it, is just as foreign to it as the artistic picturesque adornment that is so beloved in the Kantō district. Such tickets at the Shikoku temples are usually from people of Tokyo and

---

[95] In all, ten different pictures of the Daishi can be seen, of which the best-known are the following:
Mehiki Daishi – painted by himself for his mother before his departure for China.
Kōya Daishi – painted before the Daishi's death by Prince Shinnyo. Kōya Daishi sits on a priest's chair with a rosary in his left hand and a five-pronged spear in his right. Kōyasan, the three-branched fir-tree, etc, are painted as a background.

surrounding regions, or even from a wine or shōyu merchant on a pilgrimage, who, like Mr. Imazu with his masses for the souls of the flies who had fallen victims to his insect powder, combines with his pilgrimage a little advertising.

The oldest guidebooks give as the inscription on the ticket:

> Osametatematsuru Henrei Shikokuchū Reijō Dōgyō Futari

> (Pilgrimage to the holy places on Shikoku performed reverently by two travelling companions)

Today, according to the guidebook, there is written instead:

> Osametatematsuru Shikoku Reijō Henrei Dōgyō Futari

(thus, without the character chū (on) and with the transposition of the word, henrei)

Yet I have found such an abundance of variants in the tickets that I have collected that it is difficult to formulate a rule in this matter. At any rate, among the tickets that I have examined, those with the number (88) and the designation junpai instead of henrei predominate.

On the ticket-clamps there has been, on the contrary, a definite form of words preserved. Above on both sides there are usually written one or two of the ancient prayers handed down from an age preceding Kōbō Daishi:

"Great Peace under the Heavens!"

"Repose and security of the nation!"

"Repose and security of the country!"

"Repose and security of the family!"

"Prosperity to the five kinds of grain!"

"Prosperity to business!"

"Prosperity and peace for all mankind!"

"Pure sun and clear moon!"

and in addition in recent years, generally by people of the educated classes:

"World Peace!"

Under these prayers there is placed on one side the year, the day, and the month, and on the other, the name and the dwelling place of the pilgrim.

On pilgrimage for those who have died the name of the dead person is expressed by a Buddhist metaphor, e.g., "Boy of the Orchid Room", "Maiden of the Miraculous Lotus", or "The Believer awakened in the cold Time to Clarity", or even "A Woman of the Year of the Horse."

The color of the ticket is generally white; one who has made the journey more than seven times, however, gives up a red ticket; a number of times I found also green tickets, and once a dark-blue one, without being able to find out the exact significance of it. On the other hand, there are also the golden tickets of those who have gone around Shikoku as pilgrims more than fifty times.[96] Such tickets are very much sought after, since they serve as remedies against all sorts of evil diseases. Though the kindness of a priest I was able to procure such a ticket, which, it is rather remarkable to note, is sloped off above like that oldest ticket at Enmyō-ji.

A unique class is formed by the tickets which are given up by such pilgrims as go on the pilgrimage as proxies for a group of people. They are often as large as a single sheet of newspaper, and contain the names of all the members of the group. One such ticket in my possession, of a proxy sent from Hawaii, even has pictures of the Shingon temples erected in those islands.

The pilgrim leaves his ticket behind him at the various shrines of each temple, in little chapels lying along his route, in the shelters where he passes the night, as well as with people who voluntarily entertain him (see under settai). At the temples the most usual thing is to find jutting out from the wall a pointed file onto which one sticks the tickets. Often there is also a wide-meshed bamboo basket, or an invitation to throw the tickets into the chest

---

[96] According to Aibara, however: 8-21times is white, but not written upon; 22-40 times is red; 41-50 times is silver and over 50 times is gold.

for offerings. Until the most recent times, however, the tickets, insofar as they were not nailed up, were pasted on the outside of the front wall of the temple. If there was no room left, they were pasted on top of earlier ones. Sun, wind, and rain did what was needed gradually to fade out the old tickets, so that the gray-white mosaic formed in this way became not exactly a decoration to the building. It is therefore understandable that the priests are checking more and more on the disfiguration of the buildings under their management, and that one even finds such pasting-up expressly forbidden in many places. This pilgrim is as a rule glad to make use of the arrangements for receiving the tickets, for he usually carries no paste with him, but some who place a value upon duration take it with them upon the pilgrimage, and there have even been discovered specialists from the capital who take with them a writing brush with a handle of bamboo capable of being drawn out like a telescope, so that with it they can paste their tickets to the highest places, even to the ceiling of the porch.

Ticket Clamps

The ticket clamp in which the pilgrim carries his tickets consists of two simple little boards, six inches long and two inches wide, which are held together by cords and are carried hanging down from the neck over the breast. There the cords lie at the neck a straw sack about half an inch by one inch in size and a pair of relatively small *ashi-naka zōri* are tied on. These are the pack and the footgear of the Daishi, on *nidawara* and on *hakiyō*, also called *Daishi no go you*. If one takes with him such baggage and footgear for the Daishi, he will neither lack help for his journey along the way, nor have any trouble with his own feet.

In the oldest guidebooks there is also permitted instead of the ticket clamp a kind of covered box, which in contrast to our pencil-boxes opens on the small side. Whatever sort of ticket clamp one uses, the inscription remains the same:

On the front:

1st line – Great Peace Under the Heavens (Prefecture, District, City, Village etc).

2nd line – Pilgrimage to the holy places on Shikoku reverently undertaken by two travelling companions.

3rd line – Pure sun and clear moon (Name)

On the back are written:

1st line – Year

2nd line – Namu Daishi Henjō Kongō (I trust in the Daishi, the All-illuming, the Diamond)

3rd line – Month and Day

The wishes standing to the right and the left on the front were not yet specified in the guidebook Shikokkdō-Shinan.

Instead of these, year, month, and day stood on the front; name and origin on the back. In addition, over the "Namu Daishi…" and over the "Osametatematsuru…" the Sanskrit character yū was written.[97] It is striking that the old designation of the pilgrimage has been preserved unaltered on the ticket clamp – all, even the newest books, agree on this point – while on the tickets themselves such arbitrariness seems to be the rule.

One can recognize in the way that the ticket clamp is hung about the neck whether the pilgrim is making the pilgrimage in the usual or in reverse order. In the former case, the characters run from left to right; in the latter, he hangs the clamp so that the inscription is to be read from right to left.

Hand-protectors, Leggings, Seat-Apron

As a protection against the sun, the arms and hands are covered with hand-protectors, called *tekkō*[98], which reach from the middle of the forearm over the whole back of the hand. They are fastened on the underside of the arm by means of metal tongues, such as tabi have, while the

---

[97] Yū is the character (in Japanese, shuji) of Miroku Bosatsu. Perhaps the Sanskrit sign was falsely written in the old guidebooks instead of yam (in Japanese, ban), which is the character of Vairocana, the central figure of Shingon.
[98] With the doubling of the k; declared in the guidebook to be the pronunciation.

part covering the back of the hand is held in place by a loop passing over the middle finger. The hand-protectors are of white cloth, while leg-protectors, or leggings of dark cloth are also often worn. In order to protect the dress when seated, there hangs down behind from the belt, which is also of white cloth about five inches wide, a piece of cloth about the size of a Japanese hand-towel, which is called *shirishik*i, or *shirizuke*.

With that, the equipment of the pilgrim is complete. In earlier times, however, he could not start out on a journey without previously having procured a passport for himself from the village magistrate or some other official, not infrequently from the priest of his family temple. Thanks to the kindness of Professor Kageura, I have come into the possession of one such passport from the sixth year of the Bunsei Era (1823). A still older one from the Kan-en Era (1748-1751), which I was able to examine with the same gentleman, was only slightly different in tenor. Furthermore, I was able through the kindness of a young Buddhist friend to receive a sample of a passport of the Bunkwa Era (1804-1818) from the temple at Tachibana, a suburb of Matsuyama (see Supplement).

D. Upon the Journey

I. Time and Place of Departure

After the pilgrim has collected his equipment, he chooses a propitious day for his departure (*kadode*). If he lives in Shikoku, he can begin with the temple lying nearest to his home; if he comes from Kyushu, he usually takes the ship from Beppu to Uwajima and begins at the 41st temple, or he sails from Beppu or Moji to Takahama and begins with the 52nd temple, Taisan-ji, the patron temple of the province of Iyo, which according to legend was founded by a man from Kyushu. The people of Yamaguchi-ken and Hiroshima-ken also commonly begin their pilgrimages here, while those farther along toward Okayama prefer to take the short crossing to Takamatsu or Tadotsu, and, after a visit to the Konpira Shrine at Kotohira, to begin with the family temple of Kūkai, Zentsū-ji. From Kobe, Osaka and further east, the majority choose a ship which brings them to the little port of Muya, near the famous straits of Naruto.

How the requirements of the modern journey by ship and the political conditions have upset the course here to the advantage of one city and the disadvantage of other cities, we see when we turn to the old books. Since they were published in Osaka, they give information relating only to Osaka. At that time, one travelled to Tokushima and walked from there either to Bandō, in order to begin there at Reisan-ji, or to Onzan-ji (No. 18), about the same distance away, where according to tradition the bones of Kūkai's mother are interred. A second ship went to Marugame, which has lost its importance today in favor of the prefectural capital, Takamatsu, and Tadotsu, which has a better natural situation. Although this second way was 18 Japanese miles (43 English miles) longer, the fare was the same; according to the Shikokudō Shi-nan, it amounted to two monme of silver, but in the Tenpō Era to as much as four monme.

Now in all the older guidebooks there is the following rule: *"Henro no tokai: Otoko hitori, onna hitori no kumiai wa narazu, nannyo tomo ni hitori wa narazu."* (Passage of Pilgrims – One man and one woman together is not permissible; one man or one woman alone is not permissible (either).)

The reason why a man and a woman together could not travel on the boat is to be sought in the fact that on the journey the pilgrim should refrain from all relations with the other sex; whereas a single man or a single woman seems to have been generally refused in earlier times for the reason that in the case of accident there would be no one to take charge of the unfortunate one, and the owners wished to keep themselves free of unnecessary trouble with the strict police. In the Hizakurige, for example, Yajirō and Kitahachi run into difficulty through the fact that in Osaka they are requested by an unknown man in want of a travelling companion to let him join them. On the crossing to Marugame the ships runs into a storm and the man dies of seasickness. Since, however, Yajirō's and Kitahaci are his travelling companions, they must see about the disposal of his body. Today these restrictions do not of course apply. Moreover, most of the shipping companies give pilgrims a reduction of one-fifth on the price of passage.

In the early morning between two and four o'clock the ship reaches Muya. If it is in March or April, we shall meet on the ship dozens, even hundreds, of congenial travelers, who look forward with anticipation to the great adventure. Those who are making the pilgrimage for the second time are questioned about their experiences; others sing the songs of the Saikoku pilgrimage as preparation and practice for the Shikoku temples; if there is a priest among the travelers, he will probably preach a sermon on the Daishi and the blessing of the pilgrimage; and without having slept much, the pilgrims one after another step out into the cold morning air over the little gangplank. A part of them visit next the easily accessible straits of Naruto. A ferry crosses to the island of Naruto, and after a walk of one and a half to two hours a point is reached from which can be seen, as the ebb tide sets in, the thundering masses of water rushing in wild eddies to the sea through the gateway only about 1600 yards wide. This mighty spectacle of nature forms a worthy prelude to the great journey ahead. Meanwhile, others have been resting in a lodging or in the waiting-room of the steamship company, and as soon as day breaks and the cold has somewhat abated, they set out on their way towards Bando and Reisan-ji. There every pilgrim receives a printed sheet, which we can call the "Pilgrim Law" and which runs as follows in translation:

II. The Pilgrim Law

"You are requested to read this pamphlet at your leisure after you have reached your lodgings."

"Exhortation for the pilgrimage to the holy places of Shikoku"

"The pilgrim is not to veil his body in impurity nor to harbour evil thoughts in his soul; he should enter upon the penitential journey with a cleansed body and a pure heart. He should therefore during the pilgrimage strengthen others in the good way and himself also keep the ten commandments. In whatever difficulties and disagreeable situations he may find himself, he should let no thought of anger rise in him. It would be a great shame, if the journey that he has expressly undertaken in faith should come to a bad end because of some minor heed-lessness. Therefore, he should take care, in order that he may attain the fulfillment of his vow."

"Arrived at the temple, he should first perform his devotions and read the scriptures with a quiet heart, then complete the written offering without haste, and not get too far from his baggage, if there is a large crowd of people, but be very careful, since mistakes are easily made, even without evil intent. With him in his pack he should carry as little as possible, only the most necessary things, and should rather send on ahead to the address of a suitable temple what he does not need at the moment. Pocketbook, money, and the like he should under no circumstances lay down, nor should he show them to others. A box woven of reeds is preferable as receptacle for his alms. It is also recommended that he carry a special wooden rice-bowl, a teacup, and chopsticks with him. As footgear, straw san-dals are best; as a precaution, it is wise always to have an extra pair. If one wears tabi with rubber soles, one pair is indeed enough, but the feet quickly become sore on the road, and one is sure to have difficulty.

"Travelling companions, that is, those who intend to make the pilgrimage together, should assist one another lovingly and obligingly. If they meet a weak pilgrim, or one troubled with illness, they should spend themselves in caring for him as if he were their own body. That is charity after the Buddha's own heart. In the choice of 'hangers-on', by which may be understood those pilgrims who attach themselves to another, one must be cautious; one must consider that there are times when it is pleasanter to have a comrade with whom to talk than to travel alone, but that there are also occasions when our faith in a companion is betrayed. One should be especially careful of people who are always referring to their experiences as pilgrims. For there are bad people who have the most honest appearance; they approach and pretend to want to show a nearer way, to deliver efficacious prayers, or to teach one a secret magic; at the end, they only take away money form the pilgrim forcibly, and may even go so far as to violate women. Such people are to be found here and there upon the roads of Shikoku and are called 'habitues' (*jōshūsha*), ie., people who in pilgrim garb search for their livelihood on the roads of Shikoku. It is not necessary to let such people pray for one. He who merely follows the Daishi with his whole heart can attain to the granting of his prayer. One should therefore guard against such people. One should also not write one's name and dwelling too clearly on the pilgrim staff, the ticket-clamp, the tickets, and so forth, nor tell much about his personal affairs, since every year numerous people fall victims to swindling through the post office. There are signposts all along the way. Where there is no signpost, one does not go. When one comes to the lodging, one should clean his staff before washing his own feet. One should not strew his belongings all around the room, but even if it causes some inconvenience, should pack them neatly all together again. Otherwise, one will lose something, and regret afterwards is of no avail. When one leaves the shelter, one should say three times, '*On ato miyo sowaka*', and then one then one will surely not forget anything. The rule of setting out early and putting up early is as good for today as it was for earlier times. Where one is invited to stay overnight, one will surely not be badly dealt with. One should therefore turn in, even if the sun is still high. If one still wants to go on a little farther, the way often stretches out very long; before one knows it, it is late, and one does not know where to spend the night.

Shugyō, i.e., standing before the gates of strange people and asking for alms (really a reward for prayers said), is to be performed every day before about 21 houses, following the example already set by the Daishi. To do so is very good practice in forming a pious nature. One should not think he does it in order to receive money or other things; he who makes receiving the goal is only a beggar and his piety is degraded. One should consider this point well and act accordingly.

"In spring from March to May there are every-where settai, receipts of gifts of all kinds from the hands of pious people; zenkonyado, i.e., sojourn without pay in the houses of pious people; and so forth. If such favours are bestowed upon one, he should accept them in the most thankful spirit, and give his ticket in return.

"Likewise, a hasty journey taken with a heart full of business, like the *hikyaku*[99] does not lead to piety. One is only brought to shame by it, and it is therefore to be advised against. Without other intention or thought, calmly and without haste, making the pilgrimage with the prayer Namu Daishi Henjō Kongo upon one's lips – that is what the true pilgrim journey should be.

"Namu Daishi Henjō Kongō.

"Postscript: Whoever upon the pilgrimage experiences spiritual disturbances or has other cares, should turn in confidence to the priests of the pilgrimage temples. Whoever has anything to say regarding these instructions to pilgrims should kindly share it, since it concerns all pilgrims, in person or by letter with the undersigned.

"Shikoku 1st Temple Reisan-ji.

Delivered through Chizen Yoshimura."

The instructions of the little guidebooks sound the same; in many places even the tenor of the advice is exactly the same. Only in the reflections on the "ticket place", as they call the temples at which one gives up his tickets, do the books write somewhat more fully.

---

[99] The couriers of earlier days.

"When one arrives at the ticket place, he should let the betake himself with a quiet heart to the courtyard in front of the hall (the Main Hall is meant, *hondō*), draw out his ticket, and offer it to the chief divinity, cleanse himself from sinful thoughts, testify to the sincerity of his worship, and repeat some of the prayer (*ki-nenbun yori totonō*; it is therefore not stated whether all the prayers are to be said at every temple)."

III. The Prayers

Among the fifteen prayers which the pilgrim has to say, there are a Dharani-prayer, i.e., a Japanese transcription of an ancient Sanskrit prayer, and three so-called Shingon prayers, i.e., Japanese transcriptions of mantras. It is noteworthy that in the introductory prayer the word used for "emperor" is not Tennō (King of Heaven), but Tenshi (Son of Heaven); instead of this one of the newest books has Kinjō Heika (His Majesty the reigning Emperor). On the other hand, twenty-five years ago it was still the custom to say instead of the words of "of the Emperor and the Empress , of the hundred-fold civil and military offices" simply "of the Emperor and of the Shogun", even although at that time the shogun had long since ceased to be of any importance. One can understand that the people of Tosa, who were especially loyal to the Emperor, were not fond of this prayer.

Immediately below we give a translation of the prayers, or rather, the Shingon- and the Dharani- rituals in the original text. In the order of the prayers as well as in the wording of the 13th prayer slight variations appear; a newly-published but not very trustworthy guidebook even omits the passage of praise. A comparison with the daily prayers given in the canon of the Shingon sect (Shingonshū Pages), p.1535, for the faithful who have not yet given up house and family, shows agreement in form with the guidebook cited by us, *Shikoku Henro Dōgyō Futari*, by Hirota Miyoshi, except for the introduction and Prayers 8,12, and 13, which are lacking in the canon.

1. Introductory Prayer: I pray for the blessing of the chief divinity of this place, of the Daishi, of the great sun-goddes (Daijingū), of the guardian god of the province, and of all great and small divinities of Japan, of the Emperor and of the Empress, of the hundred-fold civil and military offices, of my father and of my mother, of my teachers and of my superiors, of my relatives to the sixth degree, and of my dependents and of the Dharma-world without distinction.

2. Prayer of Repentance (repeated once): The evil that I have done in times past all comes from my infinite lust, from anger and folly. Of everything that arises from body, word, and will do I now repent.

3. The Threefold Devotion (repeated three times): The dis-

ciple so-and-so surrenders himself henceforth to the Buddha, to the holy doctrine, and to the holy teachers.

4. The Three Worlds (repeated three times): The disciple so-and-so surrenders himself henceforth to the world of the Buddha, to the world of doctrine, and to the world of the teachers.

5. The Ten Commandments (repeated three times)[100]: The disciple so-and-so will henceforth not transgress:

> The commandment against wanton murder
>
> The commandment against the stealing of others' property
>
> The commandment against pitiless sensuality
>
> The commandment against willful falsehood
>
> The commandment against sinning as a consequence of indulgence in wine
>
> The commandment against gossip about neighbors' faults
>
> The commandment against conceit and slander of others
>
> The commandment against avarice that brings destruction and shame
>
> The commandment against irreconcilable wrath
>
> The commandment against ridicule and disfiguring

of the threefold treasure (i.e., Buddha, the holy doctrine,

---

[100] According to the translation by Faust-Ohasama.

and the holy teachers)

6. The Fundamental Word[101] for the Awakening of a Believing Heart (repeated three times):

On bōjishitta bodahadayami.

7. The Fundamental Word of the Sanmaya-Commandement (repeated three times):

On sanmaya satoban.

8. Praise:

If one strives after the wisdom of Buddha, one must possess a completely believing heart; simultaneously with this body, engendered by our parents, we attain the fulfillment of the great awakening.

9. The Fundamental Word of the Gloria (Kōmyō) (repeated 21 times):

Oh abokya beiroshanō makabodara manihandoma jinbara habaritaya un.

10. The Fundamental Word of Invocation to the 13 Buddhas (repeated seven times each):

a. Fudō: Nōmakusanmanda bazaradan senda makaroshada sowataya untarata kanman.

b. Shaka: Nōmakusanmanda bodanan baku.

c. Monju: On arawashanō.

d. Fugen: On sanmaya satoban.

e. Jizō: On kakaka bisanmaei sowaka

---

[101] I translate Shingon here by "fundamental word", i.e., the word that expresses the essence of a matter.

f. Miroku: On baitareiya a sowaka.

g. Yakushi: On korokoro sendari matōgi sowaka.

h. Kwannon: On arorikya sowaka.

i. Seishi: On zanzansaku sowaka.

j. Amida: On amirita teizeikara un.

k. Ashuku: On akishubiya un.

l. Dainichi of the Kongōkai and of the Taizōkai:

On abira unken bazaar dadoban.

m. Kokūzō: Nōbō akyasha kya rabaya on arikya maribori sowaka.

11. Invocations of the Daishi (repeated 21 times):

Namu Daishi Henjō Kongō

12. Dharani – Prayer of the great Kongō-wheel (repeated 7 times?):

Nōmaku shitchiriya jibikyanan tatatgyata nan an birajibiraji makashakyara bajiri satasata sarateisaratei taraitarai badamani sanbanjani taramachi shitta giriya taran sowaka.

13. Prayer (repeated once): May all grievous sins, the five deadly sins, be destroyed, that I and others in like manner may attain Buddhahood in this body!

14. Song of the particular Temple (in the guidebook mentioned here, not quoted but taken as a matter of course).

15. Intercession (ekō): We pray that this blessing may be shared by all beings We would attain the Way of the Buddha together with all others.

IV. The Written Offering (*Nōkyō*)

As a rule, the pilgrim performs his devotions at the main hall as well as the hall dedicated to the Daishi. After he has finished, he looks around for a signboard with the inscription *nōkyōsho*. *Nō* signifies "paying in, delivering, giving up"; *kyō* are the holy writings, the sutras; *sho* means "place." Therefore, *nōkyōsho* is the place where one donates or gives up the sutras. I have tried to translate nōkyō with the words "written offerings", although I feel that today this meaning is clearly understood by only a very few pilgrims. In earlier times, when the books were still written by hand and were correspondingly scarce, one was accustomed upon the pilgrimage to offer at each temple a portion of each sutra as a contribution to the library. Later, when the temples had become well-provided with scripts, it became the custom to replace one's offering of a sutra with a gift of money, which varied with circumstances, in some cases being a stipulated sum, and in others being referred to the pleasure of the pilgrim. This practice lead repeatedly, however, to disputes, such as the great dispute that Shikokuzaru experienced in the year 1901, as mentioned above, at the Tsudera in Tosa, between about two hundred pilgrims and three or four priests who had tried to overcharge them, and had answered a request for re-consideration in a very unholy way by insulting the pilgrims. Today the fee for the written offering is fixed in all temples at five sen, which with an average of 30,000 to 40,000 pilgrims a year is equivalent to a revenue of at least $750 to $800. (Translator: at a 2-1 rate of exchange.) accruing to each of the 88 temples from the pilgrimage business, quite apart from other income from gifts, burials, the sale of charms, incense, and so forth. As I have already marked above, in addition to the fee for the written offering at the Tsudera in Tosa, a further amount of ten sen for a tile for the bell-tower was asked of me. Although I passed by many temples where single buildings had been newly erected and where great stands with little tablets of wood bearing the names of pious donors showed that money was being collected, I was asked in no other place for a special gift. The newer guidebooks even mention explicitly that in the year 1924 the temples came to an agreement to put an end to offerings of that sort, which were as much extortions as they were gifts. Tsudera is therefore an exception to the rule.

One usually pays his five sen and hands a "record book of written offerings" (*nōkyōchō*) to the priest, or in most cases to the not too highly educated clerk at the window. This *nōkyōchō* is a white book about twelve inches long and eight inches wide, made of about sixty simple white or yellowish sheets of paper bound together in the Japanese way. The clerk takes the books, raises it reverently to his forehead, then lays it before him upon the low table, and after rubbing up some India ink, he paints in sweeping strokes:

1. First line: (top of page)
Kyō wo osametatematsuru (a sutra reverently offered)

2. Middle line (in very large writing):
Honson Yakushi Nyorai (to the chief divinity Yakushi Nyorai)

3. Third line (bottom of page):
Onzan-ji (or the name of the particular temple at which the offering is made)

Instead of the word Honson (chief divinity, many write one of the Sanskrit symbols referring to the divinity in question, the so-called shuji. Then the clerk reaches into the box of seals near him and presses three red seals one after the other upon what he has written: above at the right a long, narrow one with the number of the temple[102]; in the middle, one with the seal of the divinity; and below at the left a rectangular one, in most cases rather large, with the name of the temple. At this point, he takes from a small

---

[102] Instead of this there is at Temple No.60 a round seal with the character for ishi (an abbreviation for Ishizuchiyama; see p 71).

strong-box a small sheet of paper, a miniature wood-cut of the chief statue with the number and the name of the temple written on it, shoves the paper under the page on which he has just written, and with dignity and politeness hands back the book to the pilgrim, who meanwhile has made ready his white garment, and now has this also properly stamped.

The priests are generally known as excellent writers with the brush, and it is a matter of course that even the simple clerks gradually attain great skill through practice thousands and thousands of times, so that at the end of the pilgrimage the book represents a collection of the greatest interest of samples of writing. At one temple a lad scarcely ten years old made the entry for me with a sureness of touch that many an adult would have envied. It is a pity that is must also be admitted, that in the case of the absence of all scribes a large rectangular black seal, little valued by the pilgrim, is used. In famous temple like Zentsū-ji, where throughout the whole year the stream of visitors is continuous, half of the people are dispatched with such a seal, because of the lack of time to write by hand. Moreover, the color on the seals used in the nōkyō-sho is usually of German origin.

V. Settai and Shugyō

When I had finished the written offering at the 66th temple, Unpen-ji, the Temple-of-the-Region-of-Clouds, which lies 3900 feet above sea-level, and was just getting ready to leave the temple courtyard, a woman who kept a little shop with tea, cakes, straw sandals, paper, and other small wares to sell to pilgrims came upon to me and handed me a one sen piece. I did not want to receive it at first, since as a pilgrim travelling luxuriously by train and auto I considered myself entirely unworthy of the gift; besides, I had not once put on the pilgrim garments, but I had the Kongō staff in my hand. The kind woman persistently held out the money to me, saying, "Dōzo, o settai."

So at last I took it, and in my inexperience – it was towards the beginning of my journey – even forgot to leave my ticket with the happy donor, as would have been fitting. Also, when I stayed overnight in a temple for the first time, the priest returned every gift of mine the next morning with the explanation that it was *settai*. What is the real meaning of this *settai*, which is mentioned also in the pilgrim law?

The origin of the word is not entirely clear. Brinkley's Complete Dictionary and the dictionary of Genaki give under the head of *setsu* (to touch, to unite oneself with someone) and *tai* (to wait, to wait on) two meanings: 1) the reception and entertainment of guests; 2) the sharing of food and drink free of charge. No doubt with reference to these two meanings, Genkai gives as a synonym, Brinkley as an alternative writing, seyo, i.e., *se* (alms) and *yo* (to give). Bukkyō Daijiten associates settai with *shōtai* (setsu, to take, to help; tai, to wait on), which he explains in the following manner: "*Shōtai*, also read *settai*, also *moncha*, 'gate-tea': a method and a way of giving alms to priests on pilgrimage or travelling. There is placed in the road or in front of the house clear water or hot tea, and the travelers coming past, or the priests carrying on shugyō, are allowed to drink of it." If one considers that settai, as Brinkley has it, has a very general meaning, by no means limited to charity, while in Shikoku there has arisen under that name a quite definite sort of charity, which far exceeds the conception given in the explanation of Bukkyō Daijiten; if moreover one considers that until twenty or thirty years ago there were many people who wrote a little book of their experiences after the pilgrimage and distributed it without charge among their acquaintances; that such little books were called sehon (se=alms, gift; hon=book); that besides, as we have seen, settai is often paraphrased with the characters seyo; it may be asked whether settai did not originally mean setai (se=alms; tai=to wait on), as Shikokuzaru writes it many times. The doubling of a single consonant coming after a short vowel is found not merely in this case. *Edokko* is doubtless the best-known example of it, but even in the pilgrim's equipment we find a word which has doubled the consonant after e, namely, tekkō, instead of teko. The related meaning of the words setai and settai may naturally have assisted in the change; from the agreement in sound to the similarity in writing is then only a short step.

In Shikoku settai is of course not confined only to the proferring of tea. To be sure, there are temples where each pilgrim is entertained with tea; moreover, in Awa between the 21st and the 22nd temples, in a neighbourhood where much tea is grown, one can be regaled with tea to one's heart's content in every house in the village of Asabi, which stretches along for a half hour of the journey. The people invite one in to rest and to drink, as I have myself experienced. But this is only a small part of what is offered to the pilgrim as settai. Shikokuzaru once took the trouble to note down everything that he received in the course of one day, and made the following list:

Shaving	once
Toilet paper	one package
Azukimeshi (rice with red beans)	one bowlful
Cash	five rin (half a sen)
Toilet paper	one package
White rice cakes	three

Rice and millet cakes	two
Azukimeshi	one bowlful
Cash	five sen
Sweet potatoes	one bowlful
Polished rice	one go (about a cupful)
Polished rice	one go
Polished rice	one go

On the next day someone carried his pack for a distance as settai, while in Tokushima, where he was on the anniversary day of the death of the Daishi, he received so much paper that he gave away a part of it to school children, "an act whereby many a sheet of paper may have returned to the place of its origin."

The principal time in which this settai is dispensed is the spring. Later, the farmers have too much to do; the pilgrims also come less frequently then and it does not pay to make special preparations for them. In the spring, however, especially near a temple, brisk life and action prevail. Shikokuzaru writes more than once that he could not eat all that was offered to him. Upon the verandas of the farmers' houses there are to be seen women pilgrims sitting in the sun with loosened hair, while behind them kneels a girl or a woman, oiling their hair and doing it up. Upon the other side, there is an improvised barbershop, where the men have their hair cut, and are shaved. In certain villages settai is even undertaken as a community affair, and every year some families are designated by the community council to take charge of service to pilgrims. Even today in Awa there are actually rikisha-pullers who carry old or weak people for a distance on their journey as settai. One of the newer guidebooks promises to him who wishes it a kind of settai unique in the whole world, about 300 feet behind the 74th temple, where a doctor examines every Shikoku pilgrim free of charge, and gives him a "moxa"[103] treatment gratis. Even from places which lies six to nine miles off the pilgrim road come people with their gifts to the temples; even from the ends of Kyushu (Oita and Hyuga), which lie opposite the island of Shikoku, and form the Kii Peninsula there come every year boats with gifts, called settaibune.

This beautiful custom naturally arises from the same spirit which the word of Christ teaches: "Inasmuch as ye have done it unto one of the least of these my brethren, ye have done it unto me." Who feeds the pilgrim, feeds also the Daishi, who makes the pilgrimage with him. For that reason, in some neighbourhoods the woman of the house brings to one person two little plates with rice, one for the pilgrim and one for his invisible companion. There

---

[103] Burning on the skin with wormwood, used as a cure for many ills. (Translator)

are also on the pilgrim way people who sweep out their best room in the spring and prepare lodging for the pilgrims there. Such quarters are especially prized, since they are far preferable to usual lodging. They are called *zenkonyado* (*zen*=good, virtuous; *kon*=root, being; *yado*=shelter, inn), since this act of offering shelter is regarded as an especially good and worthy deed. The guidebook from as far back as the Jōkyō Era is already making used of such expressions as "*Kubokawa: Kono machi Shimamoto Shichibei yado wo kasha zenkon nasu hito ari*" (Kubokawa: In this village is Shichibe Shimamoto, a man who gives shelter and (so) practices virtue.) I have not been able to find the word settai in the old books; instead of it, the author of Shikokudō Henro Shinan writes, for example, "*Kono machi was henro wo awaremu hito ōshi.*" (In this place there are many people who have pity on the pilgrims.)[104]

One must distinguish carefully between settai and shugyō (*shu*=practice, *gyō*=conduct). While the former betokens gifts and other contributions that the people dwelling on the pilgrim road make especially in the spring as free-will offerings, the shugyō is, as we have already seen in the pilgrim law, a kind of religious practice through which the pilgrim is to be schooled in humility,

---

[104] Even today the word *nasake* (pity) is used in the sense of alms, as our word alms also goes back to the Greek eleemosyne, sympathy.

patience, and meekness, and in faith in the goodness of his fellow-creatures.[105] If it is disagreeable to be obliged to take gifts from strange people for whom we have performed no service, to whom we have no relation other than the chance meeting – it would be a sin to refuse -, it is indeed very humiliating to walk up to the doors of people whom we not only do not know, but have not even seen, and with the rosary between our folded hands, to recite our prayers, in order to awaken in the others the bodaishin, the believing heart, and to give them the opportunity to demonstrate their sympathy; for the worth of the practice, aside from its educational effect on us, lies in the fact that our fellow-man who have remained at home are aroused to compassion and through supporting the pilgrim also gain the ability to take part in the blessing of the pilgrimage. Not always, "does the gentle hand open"; often enough it remains closed as tightly as the door of the house before which one has stepped, and instead there sounds from within the brief invitation, quite lacking in politeness, "*O tōrii!*" (Go on!) If one is sent away in this manner five or six times in succession, one must be possessed of courage and faith, in order not to let himself be put out by it, but to finish the total of 21 houses which the pilgrim law gives as the most appropriate numbers for one day.

But, as one may imagine, the shugyō, even though

---

[105] This practice goes back to Gautama Buddha himself.

it is excellent discipline, has the great disadvantage of losing all too easily its character of a religious practice. The pilgrim law is quite right in its warning against carrying on the practice only for the sake of receiving something, but even if I do not carry it on for the sake of receiving anything, I do it nevertheless to induce others to give, with the result that I am the recipient. The psychological boundary line between religious practice and – lets us be frank – begging is too fine to remain clear to the simple intellect. Most of the pilgrims bring with them only about half of the supplies and cash necessary for the journey; the remainder they definitely plan to obtain through settai and shugyō. If the gifts are few, they do not hesitate at times to make a detour from the pilgrim way through out-of-the-way villages that have not yet been grazed bare. In that way also the number of 21 houses may sometimes be exceeded. Many cannot get rid of a feeling of shame. I still remember distinctly the embarrassed expression of two pilgrims in the lodging who left one morning before breakfast with the words: *"Shugyō ni kakarimasu kara saki ni shitsurei itashimasu."* (Since we are beginning shugyō now, we must be so rude as to depart first). I wondered why they were in such haste; only later did I find out that in Tosa one must begin shugyō while the people are still wearing their *nemaki* (night-clothes).

With others it is as the proverb says: "Appetite

comes with eating." In their joy over the success of their practice, they soon lost the shyness that they had in the beginning; usage gradually dulls sensibilities not especially fine otherwise, so that even refusals no longer pain them. Instead, the build up out of what should be a religious practice a refined art, of which the necessary properties are not lacking: instead of the simple, cedar staff, a long stick provided with rinds at the top which strike together at each stride; a hat as deep as possible; a loud bell; an excessively large rosary, and when possible a powerful conch-shell with red tassels; added to these, a skill in intoning the litany – yet so that one can understand no word of it – a mastery of the various voice-registers in the singing of the hymns, and above all an insolence that puts everything else in the shade. They do not leave the Shikoku road during their lifetime; the pilgrimage is their vocation. They are the *jōshūsha* (professional pilgrims) against which the pilgrim law gives warning. It is due chiefly to them, if shugyō in Shikoku has become a synonym for begging.

One of the very first day of my journey one of this species came up to me and addressed me with the words, *"O tsuresama, jun desu ka? Gyaku desu ka?* (Comrade, are you making the pilgrimage in the proper order, or in the reverse order?) After he had settled that point, he explained to me that his companion has become ill, and that they needed money for the return journey to Kyoto, and could I lend him two yen? He had the good luck to have met with a man who had not yet had much experience and who wanted to begin his pilgrimage favorably. Later, I learned to recognize the professional pilgrim in the shelter; it was in the village of Ikuino between the 19th and the 20th temples in Awa. In the little city of Tachie and in the temple of the same name the people had stared so and been so astonished by me that, even though it was comparatively late in the afternoon, I made use of the opportunity of riding which presented itself, and travelled on some distance into the mountains, about an hour and a half's journey from the next temple, Kakurin-ji. Meanwhile, night had fallen. I had inquired about an inn, and had learned two or three names, but when I reached the village of Ikuino at last, they said everywhere, "*Man-in*" (No room). Everyone sent me further, until at last at the end of the village I found one the pilgrim shelters about which I had been told. A man was standing in the entrance asking for shelter. They seemed, however, not too willing to take him in, when I stepped up, proffered my request, and also the information that I had been directed to this house. That helped. They invited us both to come in, and showed us into the room right next to the entrance. In the middle of it a great mosquito net was hung, under which lay a somewhat fat, stark naked man of about forty years old, fanning himself with a great kitchen fan. Hardly had the hostess disappeared into the kitchen when the man began to grumble: "Just now she turned away two; they weren't good enough for her; but now, when there is something to earn, she has room all at once…" The Japanese, who had been accepted with me, sat silently by the hibachi smoking a cigarette. I was close by, somewhat depressed at the prospect of having to sleep under the same mosquito net with the unfriendly, uninviting guest; but sine the old woman had not yet appeared with the evening meal, and the mosquitoes were setting upon me more and more, I took courage and slipped under the net with him. Now he became really ungracious: "You haven't been careful, but have raised the net too high. Now some have surely come in. Now we shall not be able to sleep again tonight." There-upon he drew out from under his pillow a candle and matches, struck a light, and searched thoroughly all the corners and folds of the net, continually murmuring to himself, but not finding anything. He calmed down again, lay down, and took up his former task of creating a wind. But it still worried him that we two late intruders had come, and every time that he paused a little, tired of fanning, he let fall some remark or other directed at us: "Yes, whoever has money is welcome everywhere, but poor, simple people are turned away." … "How then can five people sleep under this little net?"… "There is another room above. If the hostess hasn't another net, she shouldn't receive any more guests, or she should borrow one from somewhere."… "This has generally been a fine shelter." … "I have been in quite different ones." … "At the 5th temple, at Jizō-ji, I had it easy, with everything given to me, even biru and saida (beer and cider, i.e., effervescent lemonade), and food such as one would wish to have always." … and so on, and so on.

Still the food did not come. Listening was torture to me. In order to get him started on another subject, I asked him whether he had not made the pilgrimage often before, because he talked so much about his experiences. He answered that he had already been 22 years on the pilgrimage; he had vowed to spend 37 years in wandering about among the temples… Was he alone? … No, he wife and his child were outside in front of the house. (That was why he had spoken of five persons)… How old was his child? … Oh, just seven; wife and child he had acquired in Shikoku ("Kodomo mo kanai mo Shikoku de dekimashita.") This last fact along would have been sufficient to show that the man did not hold strictly to the pilgrim law. While he was telling me about his wife and his child, he called to them repeatedly to come in and go to bed and to sleep; otherwise, they would not be able to get up early enough on the following day. They both came in now, and the woman, who was already acquainted with the wishes and the demands of her husband, crept under the net, lying flat on the floor, but her son had not advanced far enough in acrobatics to be able to move forward like a reptile in a completely flattened condition; a part of his body still projected somewhat into the air as he got ready to slip under the net. His father snarled continually: "*Hōte kure, hōte kure!*[106] *O shiri ga takai. Hōte kure! Mata takai desu.*" (Creep! Creep! Your honorable posterior is too high. Creep! It is still too high!) And while the naked father sitting on the futon brandished the great fan with might and main, in order to keep all the blood suckers at a distance by the draught, the son crept in to us, as high or as low as might be. The absurdity of the scene and the fan of the old man had blown away from me every bit of ill-humour, and I was now entirely reconciled to having to pass the night beside the pilgrim family. But it turned out better. A young edition of the old hostess appeared, fresh from the bath, and summoned me and the guest who had come with me, disclosed as a dealer in cattle, to the upper story, where she served the simple supper, and afterwards prepared our camp under a special net.

As we woke up the next morning, we heard them in the room below already praying the long litany, interrupted at times by the tinkle of a bell. Washing arrangements were in the bath in the lower part of the house. As I came up from washing, the three were about to set out. I

---

[106] Hōte, colloquial for hatte.

asked in which direction they were travelling to the 19th or to the 20th. "To neither of them. We are going up another valley, to carry on shugyō."

The professional pilgrim is of course right in his element whenever he can assist other pilgrims in the springtime. If he belongs to the more harmless type, whose principle is "live and let live", he initiates the beginners into the art of shugyō, teaches them to overcome their original shyness in standing before strange gates, and leads them like a good shepherd to rich pastures. He teaches them that neither old people nor young married women ever give the most, but added that girls of eleven or twelve years old have the most charitable hands. He teaches them also to bow the head frankly when receiving something, and to stammer a "*katajikunaku*" (most humbly), as is seemly for the pilgrim to do. Every neighbourhood is registered and classified by him: where Shingon and Zen predominate, one receives something; Ikkōshu (=Shinshū) and Hokkeshū "*dame desu*" (no prospects). In regard to the various provinces as a whole, East Iyo and Sanuki are not so good; to be sure, the pilgrim always receives something, but mostly barley.[107] Only in Awa from the 11th temple on do conditions begin to improve, for then there is

---

[107] In earlies times the pilgrims generally received only barley, while the marionette players from Awa and the men with monkeys, most of whom came from the same province, were rewarded with rice for their entertainment.

more rice. In Tosa there is rice, to be sure, because there, in some places, there are two rice crops in a year. In the neighbourhood of Takaoka, especially, a pilgrim is never disappointed. But, as we remarked earlier, it is an important point to get up early in this province, for otherwise one is turned away. All this knowledge the professional pilgrim furnishes to the newcomer.

Often, however, he goes farther, and turns the innocence of the beginner to the latter's harm. It is a sad fact that every year dozens become victims of such deceptions as the pilgrim law warns about. It is easy to cheat the simple, pious nature; there have always been Tartuffes at all times and in all lands, and that they are not lacking on the Shikoku road does nothing to alter the fact that yearly tens of thousands return from the pilgrimage with great benefit to body, soul, and spirit. It can likewise not be denied that the custom of settai and of shugyō have had and still have a far-reaching influence upon the folk-character of the people of Shikoku, and it is only with regret that one recognizes the first sign of the changing times in the signboard that I found in Awa between the 20th and the 21st temples on the ferry over the Nakagawa, to the following effect: "You are courteously requested to abstain from making requests for gifts, begging, subscriptions for temples, and the like, since we must raise 120,000 yen for road-building."

VI. Journey on Foot.

He who wishes to receive the greatest good from the pilgrimage must naturally take the entire journey on foot. The ferry is permitted only at places where the rivers cannot be crossed on foot, as at the Yoshinogawa and at the Nakagawa in the province of Awa, as well as at the entrance to the Bay of Urato and in the Bay of Inoshiri in Tosa, and later at the Shimatogawa; and in addition to these, on a stretch of two or three Japanese miles (from five to seven and a half English miles) between the 36th and the 37th temples, where in earlier times the way was considered most difficult and most dangerous. Those who cannot walk hobble along as well as they can on crutches, and those to whom even that is no longer possible let themselves be drawn around in cripples' carts by relatives.[108] I saw only a few lepers, and these chiefly at Ishite-ji near Matsuyama, and at some well-known temples in Sanuki. Shikokuzaru declares that 25 years ago he took with him a bag containing 1000 one-mon coins, one of which he gave to every leper he met; and since at the conclusion of his journey he had only 134 coins left, he must have met 866 lepers.

---

[108] In his radio lecture in Tokyo on March 27, 1928, Aibara told of cripples who bind around the stumps of their limbs such straw sandals as are used on the hoofs of cattle, and so make the pilgrimage.

It is estimated that about seven-tenths of all pilgrims make the long journey on foot, according to the written instructions. People who are good walkers can cover the distance of about 750 miles in five weeks. Usually one counts on forty to sixty days. If rainy days come, or if the shugyou leads one by a roundabout way, it can easily take longer, especially in the case of women. The woman mentioned above, going around with an old woman of 77 years who insisted on going on foot over even the stretch between the 36th and the 37th temples allowed by the Daishi, needed as many as 100 days. In earlier times the expenses of a day's journey were reckoned as the equivalent of a *shō* (about two quarts) of unbulled rice. Today expenses are higher and the guidebook estimates that after arrival in Shikoku about a yen a day must be allowed. This may seem low to the Western reader, but it must be considered what it means to the ordinary simple people, in addition to having to give up whatever they might have earned in one or two months, to raise 30 to 60 yen, for the pilgrim is accustomed to take about that much with him on the journey. Nevertheless, I have quite often found the red ticket, indicating a pilgrimage undertaken for more than the seventh time. I could not find more recent statistics about pilgrimages several times repeated, but Shikokuzaru makes the following statements, taking his facts from a book of the year 1900, *Shikoku Reijō Junpaijin Bantsuke*

(Succession of Pilgrims to the Holy Places of Shikoku):

> Over 7 and under 20 pilgrimages – 402 persons
> Over 20 and under 30 pilgrimage – 72
> Over 30 and under 50 pilgrimages – 40
> Over 50 and under 100 pilgrimages – 16
> Over 100 pilgrimage – 14

In the above statistics, the three highest scores are 199, 170 and 168 pilgrimages. Kanikumo claims, however, to have seen a signboard erected in memory of a certain Mobei Nakatsukasa from the village of Mukuno, district of Oshima, Suō Province, who had made the pilgrimage 254 times.

Among those who have gone around Shikoku more than 100 times and who are mentioned by name by Shikokuzaru are two women, and there are the same among the pilgrims who have gone around more than 50 times. Since it is certain that these statistics do not go very far back, and since 28 years have passed since they were compiled, it is not difficult to imagine that the actual numbers must be much larger. For instance, the 85-year-od Mrs. Arai, mentioned above, has made the pilgrimage 55 times; another instance of which I know personally is that of a man who lost his relatives in the great earthquake of 1923, and who since that time has visited the temple uninterruptedly for the salvation of their souls. What those who take such a series of pilgrimage think of it, and how it is no pure enjoyments to them, can be seen from the answer which Mrs. Arai gave to Mr. Tomita when he questioned here about her impressions: *"O Shikoku mo nisan do gurai kekkō desu, amari wakarisugite wa…"* (The Shikoku pilgrimage is quite fine for two or three times, but when one come to know it too well…) And then she was silent.

The golden pilgrim ticket that I possess came from a wealthy merchant in Osaka who, like the haiku-poet from Tokyo mentioned earlier, made the pilgrimage once each year. It would therefore be false to assume that all who repeat the pilgrimage belong to the class of professional pilgrims.

If circumstances do not permit one to make the entire journey on foot, there are opportunities everywhere for riding. In Iyo and in Sanuki the railroad can be used repeatedly; in Awa the temples lie close together, but there also the pilgrim can climb into a train in two places, while farther over towards Tosa, where the temples are separated by longer distances, he meets with automobiles. Tosa is the poorest of the four provinces of the island in railroads, but for that very reason it has the best auto roads, and a corresponding thick net of auto lines. In the southern part of Tosa, moreover, a sea-route can be chosen instead of the overland route, even though it may be on unsteady boats, where embarkation is frequently not lacking in excitement. On the whole, it is possible to travel over two-thirds of the distance with the help of all kinds of conveyances, from the jolting old *basha* (horse-drawn wagons) to the elegant Buicks, from the old, worn-out river ferries to the not less old, but somewhat roomier coastal steamers. Who therefore lays his plans well, so that he always makes good connections at the junctions, can visit all the temples in about three weeks. I myself visited eight temples lying on the outskirts of Matsuyama in two days before and after my actual journey; and the remainder in the time between July 12th and August 5th, 1927; and even out of that time I returned once to Matsuyama for four days. If I had taken the journey as a whole, I could have finished it in 23 or 24 days. Even with the use of conveyances, the journey, especially in summer, is strenuous enough, since, as one can easily imagine, the most difficult parts of it must be done by foot. The city resident from Osaka or from Kyoto would search in vain for beautiful roads such as those leading up Kōyasan or Hieizan, as well as for the people to push him from behind up the steep mountains, which as he is used to on the temples mountains just named. When it is remembered how rough and stony most of the mountain paths are even today, some idea can be gained of what hardships the pilgrim had to face in earlier centuries, when the country was still almost entirely closed.

VII. Wood Money Inns

All this could, however, be more easily borne, if there were at least a certainty of finding good quarters every evening, where recovery from the exertions of the day could be made. Admission into private houses, the zenkonyado, belongs in the category of rare good luck. Somewhat more frequently there is the opportunity of spending the night in a temple. About a quarter, at the most a third, of the 88 temples are prepared to give lodgings to pilgrims. Some of them, especially those, such as Unpen-ji, situated on high mountains, have a great hall, used for overnight shelter, called tsūyado, which, however, is quickly filled to capacity in times of great crowds. The quarter, therefore, to which most pilgrims, for good or for ill, must have recourse each evening is the wood-money inn, the kichinyado, called also in student language with grim humour in elegant half-Chinese, half-European language Mokuchin Hoteru, "Motel Wood Money." The name comes from the fact that in earlier times the guest in such an inn brought his rice or his barley with him, and gave it to the host or the hostess to cook. In recompense for the necessary firewood, he had to pay a fixed sum, for which he received tea with his rice and a small amount of vegetables as a side dish. Shelter for the night was entirely free. Even today the pilgrim can give to the host for cooking the rice or the barley that he has received during the day as settai or through shugyō. One usually hands over only as much as one wishes to have cooked. For a gō (about a cupful) of rice a tariff is fixed, which varies, however, with the place and the time of year, of between nine and a half and twelve and a half sen, and according to that the bill is reckoned. The rice that has not been eaten is packed up in little provision basket for lunch by the wayside.

There can of course be no talk under such circumstances of especially luxurious lodging. The ingredients are mostly some little slices of pickled radish or eggplant, lily roots, or salt plums. Slices of cucumber in vinegar with some onions are considered quite a tidbit, but if the charge is high, they provide also a hot soup with a few pieces of fu, some onions, and a few beans in it.[109]

The futon are what one calls in Japan *senbei-futon*, that is, through generations of sleepers who have lain upon them they have become as thin and hard as the Japanese waffles. Besides, most of them are so short that even a Japanese cannot stretch out at full length upon them. On cold March nights neither the upper nor the lower futon affords enough protection against the cold, but this is

---

[109] Fu is a kind of bread made of wheat flour, which is used in soup and in many other ways.

compensated for by having people lie so close together in the narrow room that they keep each other warm. Aside from the fact that many pilgrims arrive late in the evening, and others leave at the break of day after they have performed their devotions before the tokonoma with the ringing of bells, rubbing of rosaries, and recital of prayers, the night's rest is not disturbed. What a student wrote me about a night in a wood-money inn also applies: "Then the louse, the flea, and the tick come, and bite you." Shikoku-zaru calls it the settai of the kichinyado. Especially at the time of the great crowds in the spring months, one cannot avoid picking up some vermin along the way, and one will understand that the Japanese, who loves cleanliness so, must feel it an insult to his body to be obliged to pass the night for weeks at a time in such dirty inns, a humiliation that he takes upon himself for the sake of the Daishi. "After all, no one has yet died because of a louse," once said a pilgrim, a merchant from Osaka, to me, when we were speaking about this nuisance of the wood-money inns. Indeed, the free life in the out-of-doors and the spiritual condition of the pilgrims gives them an immunity towards those conditions injurious to their health that they expect to meet with, an immunity such as was also observed in the frontline trenches during the World War.

In the section on *shugyō*, I have already spoken of an evening in a wood-money inn. Here, as a supplement to that, is a picture of my first night in such an inn. Although I undertook the pilgrimage in the summer, which is poor in pilgrims, the reader will nevertheless get some idea of how the evening of a pilgrim passes.

The day had been very hot and exhausting. I had spent the previous evening in an inn in Kotohira, had visited Zentsū-ji once more in the morning, in order to take some more photographs, and had then taken the electric train to the 76th temple, Konzō-ji, which had served the Marshal Nogi as a dwelling when he was still the commander of the regiment of Marugame, and where today a pine-tree, *"Nogi Taishō no Tsumagaeshi matsu."* (The pine tree where General Nogi sent his wife home), recalls the episode of how the wife of the colonel, who was in the capital and longing for her husband, came to visit him, but was sent home by him when evening came with the words: "It is already late, so you had better go home now." In the next temple at Tadotsu the wife of an attorney in Shanghai spoke to me. She had lived in England for three years, had gone on the Shikoku pilgrimage in the previous year, and now had come back to that place for the summer. After a short train trip, I had behind me the journey in the midday heat from the 78th temple to the salt fields of Sakaide, and had passed through the long-drawn-out little city of the same name to the 79th temple, where there was the clear spring in which the coffin of the Emperor Sutoku stood for months, keeping cool until instructions for entombment were received from the capital. Today a pleasant woman, who had set up a little booth under a canopy, was cooling her lemonade and her tokoroten cakes in the same spring. Like most of the pilgrims, I went from here to the 81st temple, which was remarkably well cared for, as it was the former site of the grave of the Emperor Sutoku. A broad road, interrupted at intervals of 150 or 300 feet by beautiful granite stones to make the ascent easier, led gradually to the top of the mountain, where the temple buildings were scattered about under magnificent cryptomerias and other old trees. It was already quite late in the afternoon when I sounded the old bell under the bell-tower, upon whose roof a kiri-tree was growing, and then walked on along the ridge of the mountain to the 82nd temple, Negoro-ji. On the way I passed by a hut, which, situated as it was in the middle of the woods, served the pilgrims in the spring as a shelter, but was now closed. Yet two pilgrims had already settled themselves to rest on the open veranda. It was dusk when I finally reached Negoro-ji. Just outside the gate there stood at the left against the mountainside a wood-money inn, upon whose veranda three pilgrims were already sitting, taking off their sandals. In front of the inn there were a small plateau with another lower bank jutting out from its steep side. In front of the this the trees were thinner, so that one could glimpse the Inland Sea at one's feet, with Takamatsu and the simple silhouette of the Yashima Peninsula ("House Island") which resembles a Japanese house with its flat outline of roof. I asked if they accommodated guests overnight in the temple. No, they said, they were not prepared to do so, but the nearest inn was at least an hour's journey away, and hard to find in the darkness; I had better spend the night there. Up to that time, I had had good luck, staying twice in temples, twice in inns, and once in the home of one of my students. Now for the first time I was to make the acquaintance of the wood-money inn.

One of the pilgrims already there, a man with a very fine face and gold-rimmed spectacles, who made a thoroughly fine impression in speech and behaviour, asked the hostess who was busy in the kitchen, whether I could stay overnight. She said that I could, and immediately sent a young girl out to take my staff, wash its point, and place it with the others in the niche. In this niche a picture of Buddha was hanging. My first predicament came when they informed me that the bath was ready. Up to this time I had received a bath kimono everywhere; here I discovered that the pilgrims had their own with them in their packs. I therefore left my clothes in the room and betook myself in Adam's costume through the dark kitchen to the bath, which, as everywhere in Japan, one expects to find as a matter of course in even the smallest inn. Here it was an iron kettle, set into a niche in the rock. By groping around in the space in front of it, I discovered a match-box and a small stump of a candle, which was stuck to the stone. When I lighted it, I saw that the ceiling and the walls were black with candle soot. The bath water did not seem entirely clean to me, but it did well enough to wash away the dust and the sweat of the hot day. Besides, after the bath the girl brought me fresh water to rinse off with. When I returned to the room, the hostess was already there to ask me how much rice she should cook. The second predicament! Out of which the man with the gold-rimmed spectacles helped me as he briefly ordered five gō for me. How should I have known how many gō of rice I was able to consume? Since then, I have learned that for a European two or three gō for the evening or the morning meal are quite enough, while in contrast to this I met a pilgrim in Tosa who had a *shō* (ten *gō*) cooked for himself alone, which of course furnished his day's provisions.

Meanwhile a new pilgrim came in, a many of a young and fresh appearance, and I now discovered all that I had previously omitted doing. After he had politely asked the hostess for shelter, he washed his staff and then entered the room, where he first placed the staff with the others, while, if I recall correctly, he called several times on the name of the Daishi. Then he unpacked a small portable shrine to Buddha, which he carried attached to his pack[110] and for about ten minutes said his prayers before it, sounding his bells at intervals. Only after he had finished this, did he come to the side of the room where we sat and greet us in the most polite way, about as follows: "It is very fine that you are making the pilgrimage.[111] Pardon me, please, for disturbing you, and allow me to be your companion for this one night." Since the newcomer declared that he wished no rice, it was not long before they brought us our meal. Every guest received a small bucket with rice, and a simple red tray on which stood a bowl with some hot soup and fu, as well as a little plate with some slices of pickle. In accordance with his request, the latest comer received only the tray with some hot water, which he had ordered. I asked where the rice-bowl was. They were all amazed at my question as they all went to their packs to get their own! Apparently, one must furnish one's own. The man with the gold spectacles immediately calls the hostess and asked her if she will lend me a rice-bowl. I scoop out some rice for myself and look for the chopsticks. Astonishment again, and the question at what temple I

---

[110] Probably with a figure of the Daishi, in order to more exactly symbolize the "Pilgrimage of Two."

[111] *Yō o mairi de gozaimasu*. This is a greeting that the pilgrims are accustomed to exchange in passing, and that might be translated somewhat more freely by "Welcome to the pilgrimage!" or "Success to your pilgrimage!"

began my journey! Again my mentor interposes before I have time to ask the hostess. Meanwhile, the others have unpacked their own eating utensils, and in silence, though not noiselessly, the meal proceeds. Only when the young man who has previously declared that he wants no rice takes three spoonfuls of a light-water powder from a little bag and begins to stir it up with warm water can the others not suppress their curiosity, and ask him what he has there to eat. "*Mugi no ko*" (barley flour)[112]; that is his *shingwan* (the real wish of his heart, a vow taken here for the fulfillment of this wish). In the spring of the previous year he had fallen seriously ill with stomach trouble; he had recovered on the pilgrimage; had made the journey again to express his thanks, and had come again to Shikoku this year on a pilgrimage of thanksgiving, on rei-mawari. Everyone admired the lively young man, who, as I could judge for myself the next morning, ran over the mountains as nimbly as a weasel.

After the meal was finished, the trays were carried away, but the rice-bowl everyone kept with him and put into his pack. Then the visitors' book was passed around.

---

[112] The meal, the so-called *hattaiko*, was of course roasted, and was therefore yellow; on the other hand, the buckwheat meal of the hermits (sennin) is enjoyed to this day raw, simply mixed with a little cold water. In the novel Shukumei by Iwasaburō Okino, a little bag of *hattai* forgotten by a pilgrim in free lodgings (*zenkonyado*) is seized and held by the police as gunpowder when they search the house.

While the others were registering in it, everyone took out of his ticket-clamp as many tickets as he would probably need on the following day, and filled them out. One of the pilgrims then studied his guidebook, and I chatted with the man who had helped me in such a friendly way. I dared not ask on the first evening what had brought him to Shikoku; I learned only that he came from Tokyo and had been prevented through various business transactions from making the pilgrimage in the spring, as he had intended to do. Meanwhile, the oil lamp had been taken down from the middle of the room and fixed to the cross-beam between our room and the small open room that led to the kitchen. The thin, short futon and the pillows woven of rushes were brought in and spread down. It was worthy of notice that upon the under-futon a piece of rush mat was laid[113], I suppose so that one might be cooler when lying on it. Behind our room lay another into which three persons had already gone. The young man who had come in last and the man from Tokyo had remained while the beds were being spread. For all of us three a great net was at last spread out and we guests helped the host in hanging it. But before we lay down, the bill had to be paid: a gō of rice cost nine and a half sen, so my bill for the night

---

[113] I have since heard that these mats are also used in the houses of peasants. Perhaps they make it harder for the fleas to jump about.

amounted to 47.5 sen. The man from Tokyo pointed out that money for tea or for a tip was not necessary. The man who was living on a diet of meal paid about 20 sen. That night I was troubled very little by vermin. The ants that had bothered me during the meal seemed luckily to be interested more in our viands than in us. On the other hand, a few mosquitos found their way in under the net, either through holes or at some time when the wind lifted a corner from the floor.

Later on, I frequently had to spend the night in wood-money inns. Since it was summer, and there were therefore few guests, I got by rather well, as far as vermin were concerned. Nevertheless, the desire to continue the journey left me for several hours when one morning after leaving one such inn I discovered a well-nourished body-louse on my small Japanese towel. I was also told in Tosa that the fear of vermin is the reason why in this province no one who carries a pilgrim staff is received into an inn or a hotel, for it is said that other travelers stay away from an inn that is patronized by pilgrims. In the other three provinces also it happens at times that a pilgrim is turned away from an inn. He therefore who does not possess enough pilgrim courage to stay in the wood-money inn first deposits his pack and his staff there, changes his clothes, and then, riding in a rickshaw if possible, looks for a hotel. And yet, one finds everywhere except in Tosa inns that carry on in the same building or in two neighbouring buildings the business of furnishing pilgrim lodgings and of sheltering ordinary people in an inn. In such inns one can obtain better lodgings without wholly getting out of the pilgrim atmosphere.

VIII. Fasts

If one puts up at an inn that carries on such a two-fold business, the first question after one has been shown to this room is: "*Dannasan wo shōjin desu ka? Dō desu ka?*" (Is the gentleman fasting or not?) Fasting is a customary part of the true pilgrim journey. The Buddhist conception of fasting is, as you know, much more severe than the Catholic-Christian idea: no sort of animal food is partaken of, and this includes even fish, eggs, and such things. It is also a matter of course that the pilgrim should abstain from intoxicating drink. How one manages, in regions that that many other pilgrims as guests, as well as the true Shikoku pilgrims, not entirely to deny himself the beloved sake, the following conversation that Shikokuzaru had in Kotohira with the maid of the inn will show: "*Danna, gomazu was ikaga desu ka?*"… "*Gomazu wa nan desu ka?*" … "*Oya, danna o hendo de hajimete da to meiru.*" … "*Shireta koto yo. O hendo wa shōbai ni shite otte tamaru ka?*" … "*J ate, anata gomazu no shiraide amari desu yo. Osasa desu yo.*" (Would the gentleman care for goma-vinegar? Gome-vineger? What is that?.. Aha! I can see that the gentleman is making the pilgrimage for the first time.. Naturally. Do I look as if I made a business of going on pilgrimage?...No, not at all, but you ought to know goma-vinegar. It is rice-wine, don't you see?)

Mr Tomita even had a cup of rice-wine pressed upon him in a temple, with a reference to one of the last exhortations of the Daishi: "*Onshu ippai kore wo yurusu.*" (I allow one cup of warm wine.) The "small cup" that was offered to him was at least as large as a large teacup. As a German, I was repeatedly offered beer, even for breakfast, in the temples where I spent the night, for this drink, according to middle-school textbooks, takes the place of tea with us. In the wood-money inns, on the other hand, I never found rice-wine, nor saw anyone drinking it. Even if the pilgrim should take a sip of sake here and there, he must do without enough else, and many a longing glance falls upon the sharks' fins, the cuttle-fish, and the bonito, as they hang drying everywhere in the Tosa ports or lie in kilns in the sun; or in Iyo upon the fresh fish from the Inland Sea, which are for sale everywhere and are acknowledged as the best in the country.

Just think what a temptation it is for the people who come from distant regions to Shikoku – perhaps for the only time in their lives – and travel through the country

214

for weeks, to see before their eyes the beautiful things[114] of which they have heard, and yet not be allowed to enjoy them! It will be readily admitted that it is quite understandable for some here and there to fall victims to temptatation, and it will be felt that the instructions and their observance are humbug because there are shadows as well as sunshine. Just as today seven out of every ten pilgrims still cover the whole way on foot, although even in the nōkyōsho of the temples information is given about ways and means of conveyance, by far the greater number today still adhere strictly to the law, and are ready at the first opportunity to criticized those who break it. He who assumes staff and costume must submit to the law. Certain temples are even regarded as ohenro on sekisho (pilgrim barriers), where misfortune overtakes the impenitent among them as a sign of heavenly punishment, whether it be that adulterous women are caught by the hair there in the rope of the temple bell, or that bad men are struck dead by the hurtling down the huge bell. That power and riches are worth nothing either, but are a hindrance to the wealthy Shikoku pilgrim, as they were also to the rich

---

[114] The so-called *meibutsu*, products that are made in a particular place in a special district, and enjoy a celebrity equal to that among us of pretzels from Speyer, Lebkuchen fron Nurnberg, Handkase from the Harz, Westphalian ham, sprats from Kiel, Munich Beer, and so forth. (Or in the USA, California oranges, Boston codfish, Idaho potatoes, Wisconsin cheese, Oregon apples, Virginia ham, and so forth. Translator)

young man in the Bible, can be seen from the following tale, which people on the pilgrimage recount:

"The rich Kichizaemon Sumitomo, the founder of the banking firm that is world-renowned today, and to which belong also the copper mines of Besshi in Shikoku, decided one day to undertake the pilgrimage to the 88 temples. As was fitting for such a wealthy man, he equipped a large company to go with him. With many servants and other followers besides, he travelled in a se-dan-chair form place to place, and put up at only the best inns and hotels, where he was received ceremoniously and entertained in festive fashion. When he came to the tem-ples, he scarcely set foot outside the sedan-chair, while one servant jumped to make the written offering, and another to give up the ticket and to offer the prayers. The pilgrim-age was thus made very comfortably and smoothly. When he had returned to Osaka, however, and his friends came to hear about his journey, he wanted to show them also the nōkyōchō, the book with the entries and seals received for the written offerings A servant brought the book. Ki-chizaemon opened it to the first page – it was blank! He turned over the leaves, but no matter where he looked, every page was blank, to the great astonishment of his guests and to his own painful confusion. Yet the lesson was effective. In a great secrecy he got ready again for the journey, and travelled a second time through the four

provinces as a simple, unknown pilgrim, enduring all difficulties and privations, and when he came home this time
and opened his book, all the characters were clear and
fresh, and the seals shone as they had at the time that he
had received them."

IX. Women on the Pilgrimage

While women in earlier times in Europe held a
subordinate place in the church (mulier taceat in ecclesia!),
the general condition of affairs today is that she takes a
greater part in church life than the man. Especially in the
case of pilgrimages, as for example that to Lourdes, there
are to be met as a rule more women than men. In Japan
also, in Buddhism (and in general), women in earlier times
stood one stage lower than men; if she was to attain to
Buddhahood, it was made more difficult for her than for
men. Upon the Shikoku pilgrimage today the two sexes are
about equally divided. The old books do not mention what
the condition was earlier, but women's figures are to be
seen in all pictures, and furthermore, the instructions say
that we may conclude that there must have been women
pilgrims also in early times. Today it is no longer unusual
to see young girls making the pilgrimage alone. According
to Shikokuzaru, the girls from Awa are the most numerous,
because one of the former daimyo of that place, Koroku

Hachisuka, was a very pious Buddhist, and his example had a great influence upon the people. Since that time, the inhabitants of Awa have been said to be very pious, so that the parents send their daughters on the pilgrimage when they reach the marriageable age. The Daishi is considered there to be of some value also as a helper in marriage (*musubi no kami*, god of union). Quite otherwise is it in Tosa, where the Daishi does not stand so high in public opinion. When a maiden of the provinces goes to the 88 temples, all the neighbours and soon the whole village ask the same question: "What serious disease has she, I wonder?" and prejudice against the entire family is aroused.[115]

Transgressions and improprieties may often happen when the pilgrims lie so thickly together in the lodging, so that the saying "*tatami no heri ga kunisakai*" (the edge of the mat is the boundary of the province) is no longer worth anything. He who knows the history and the conditions of pilgrimages in Germany knows that there too thing were not always above criticisms. One must guard against seeing the shadows here blacker than they are in reality.

In German geography books, even in those which

---

[115] In various provinces outside of Shikoku it seems that it is no recommendation even for men to have been on the Shikoku pilgrimage. It is said that in Yamaguchi Prefecture there is often objection to a certain family at the time of discussions about marriage, for however good and well-off they may be, the grandfather, or somebody or other, once went on a pilgrimage to the 88 temples.

have appeared since the World War, one can read that the ascent of Mount Fuji is forbidden to women. This prohibition was abolished decades ago, as was a similar one concerning other mountains, among which is Kōya, founded by Kōbō Daishi. This prohibition to women may be scribed to the transgressions and excesses that were connected with the tantristic rites[116], as it has been proved that they were carried on in earlier times, as for example on Kōya. Today with a few exceptions such prohibitions have been relaxed, and yet, Mount Nantai (man's body) at Nikko is to this day open to women only during a few weeks in the summer, and even then the women must abide by certain rules. The balance of the prohibitions to women have been preserved on the Shikoku pilgrimage in two places, which, as may well be imagined, are in conservative Tosa and in Iyo at Maegami-ji, which is connected with En no Ozunu and Shugendō. There is a pilgrim poem that runs as follows:

> Shikoku megutte
> Yukarenu tera wa
> Tosa de Nishidera to Higashidera

---

[116] Judging by all appearance, these rites entered the Shingon teaching through Shugendō.

The temples to which one (as a woman)
cannot go on the trip around Shikoku
are the Nishidera and the Higashidera in Tosa

Twenty-six years ago, when Kōya had long been open to women, Shikokuzaru found a sign still posted half-way up the mountain on the way to the Higashidera (No.24): "*Kono tokoro nyonin kinsei ni tsuki nyonin wa migi ni yukubeshi.*" (Since this place is forbidden to women, women have to go to the right.) He found a similar sign in front of the 26th temple, Nishidera. Today entrance to both temples is permitted to women, but there is still a place at the entrance to the temple yard of Nishidera, where the guidebook instructs men to go to the right and women to the left. On the other hand, Maegami-ji in Iyo has, as we have already noted above, one main hall for men and another for women.

While there are still a few places in Tosa and in Iyo forbidden to women, the holy of holies in the 65th temple, the splendid Kinkōzan Senryū-ji in Iyo, is an institution of Kōyasan, and, according to legend, was assigned to women to Kōbō Daishi as a compensation for Kōya, which was forbidden to them. Therefore, the entrance to women to this temple was allowed from the beginning. Even today the temple is called the Women's Kōya.[117]

---

[117] There is at least one other temple with this designation,

X. The Songs, Go Eika

To the worship that the pilgrim performs at each temple there belongs also the chanting of a little spiritual song called *go eika*, one of which is given for each temple in the guidebook, and which refers in some way or other to the location of the temple. These songs are all rather old, as can be seen from the fact that even where the name of the temple has been later changed, as in the case of Ishite-ji and some other temples, the original name lives on in the song, although the meaning of the allusion contained in it has been lost. Meanwhile, there is no doubt that the songs of the 33-Kwannon temples of Saikoku have furnished the model for those of the 88 Shikoku temples. Not only do the former, without exception, rank higher in poetical worth, but also their melody has "set the fashion" for Shikoku. In order to understand the difference in poetical content, lets us compare two typical songs, such as the one from the Shosha in the province of Harima and that of Taisan-ji, the chief temple of the province of Iyo. The latter is perhaps not especially bad, being about average, yet most of them, because of the plays on words contained in them, do not lend themselves easily to translation.

---

namely, Kongō-ji, in Nagano in Kawachi Province.

Harubaru to
Noboreba Shosha no
Yamaoroshi
Matsu o hibiki mo
Mi nori naruran.

    As from the distance we come near to Shosha
    Down from the mountain swiftly a breeze soughs
    Through the dark forest; the echoing pine boughs
    Sound in our ears like the precepts of Buddha.

Taisan wo
Noboreba ase no
Idekeredo
Nochi no yo omeba
Nan no ku nashi

    As you climb to Taisan-ji,
    Oh, how the sweat pours out!
    But just think of the future world,
    And put all pain to rout!

The method of singing is a rather long-drawn-out chanting, in the course of which a decided accent must fall on each of the 31 syllables. Every line is divided into two parts with a breath between them. The melody is in a major key and has a very pleasing effect when performed by a good singer.

There are groups, the so-called Kwannonkō, that have made it their task to foster the go eika. In Shikoku they flourish in the greatest numbers in Iyo in the neighbourhood of Matsuyama. In that city alone there are about twenty such companies. The people meet once a month, usually in a temple, and sitting devoutly before the altar of Buddha sing through once the songs of the 33 Kwannon temples. That these songs exclusively are sung at such a time is further proof of the fact that they are the model for all others. From time to time a great sing-ing-match takes places. Last year I visited such a match in a temple in Tachibana, a suburb of Matsuyama. The nephew of the priest had invited me, and so I appeared in the first hour of the afternoon. As I drew near to the temple, there was already a remarkable ringing and singing in the air that I could not entirely understand. In the priests' dwelling the sliding walls between the three largest rooms had been taken out, and thus a single great hall created. Since it was still as warm as in summer, all the shōji had been removed, so that the glance could sweep unhindered over the beautiful garden at the side of the dwelling. At the farther end of the crowded hall was a row of tables, behind which about twelve men sat, two of them were priests. Five of them were the judges, and had already been discharging their duties without a break since early morning. Somewhat in the foreground on the right stood a single table, behind which the competing singers had to take their places. One could sing either standing or sitting. First, everyone recited the stereotyped introduction: "*Osametatematsuru Saikoku sanjūsankasho dai … ban…no kuni…yama (or …tera)*" (I reverently offer (the song) of the such-and-such temple of the 33 places in Saikoku, the …yama (or … dera) in the province of …), at the conclusion of which he began the real song in a different voice. The singer could not choose a favourite song, but had to perform the song next in order in the succession. The judges played the same role as the markers among "Meistersinger": they had to consider whether the singer gave a sufficient number of accents to each syllable, whether he struck the bell at the right place, whether he got out of breath, whether he was guilty of any impurities in voice or melody, and so forth. Each of them could award a fixed number of points, the highest in our case being 80. Then the singer had finished, the points of the judges were added, and the result was immediately painted with India ink upon a great sheet of paper, which was hung upon a pillar before the eyes of all. Whoever reads a syllable falsely, even though it be only beginning inadvertently with "a" in such a word as the name Ōmi, which is written in kana "a-u-mi"; whoever loses his breath or has the misfortune to omit a bell-stroke or to give one in the wrong place; is through with singing, and must retire amid general laughter without being allowed to sing in the end. One after another the two or three hundred participants sing their songs; then the best are separated out and sing again; and so on and on, until finally the prize winner is determined. People come and go, the judges are served refreshments, but the singing goes on uninterruptedly. Close by in the kitchen two are practicing; another is in the temple hall and is rehearsing there before the statue of Kwannon; outside in the courtyard a noodle-seller has set up a small booth out of which the "osametatematsuru" sounds; in all the neighbouring houses, not excluding the bath-house with its especially good acoustics, people are practicing their singing; yes, even as I went late in the evening over the bridge that leads back to the city and is several hundred yards away from the temple, I distinguished the tones now well-known to me; for even at about midnight the singing-match had not ended, but lasted until about eight o'clock the following morning. Only then was the last battle decided and until then the awarding of the prize had to wait, and the same melody, even it not the same words, had to be gone over about 500 times.[118] Among those who took park in the contest there

---

[118] There are two styles of singing, the usual eika-style, which is the older, and the *donkai* (literally – sip of the sea), which has a

were also women, of whom those who sang when I was present were quite successful. On the pilgrimage, however, I heard the go eika sung very seldom, although there are prescribed in the guidebook, but this may have been due to the poor time of year at which I took the journey.

XI. Votive pictures, Charms, Medicines, Yakuyoke

If one comes to Ishite-ji near Matsuyama, he will find a rather long covered passage leading from the street to the temple courtyard. At one end stands a gigantic old pine-tree, at the other the beautiful, two-storied temple-gate. On the ceiling and on the posts of this passage hang a great number of votive pictures in the most varied forms and stages of completion, among which there are even some woven of straw. Most of such pictures, as the inscription state, are presented out of gratitude for answers to prayer. They are to be found at each of the 88 temples, and are not limited to Shikoku. They are found in the greatest numbers, however, in the hall of the Daishi. Various temples have their specialties. At some temples one finds many long rolls sewed of cloth, which have been presented by women. At the 75th temple, and in still greater numbers at the 43rd, I found imitations of women's breasts made of white cloth, in one case finely mounted on a board

quicker melody, less in harmony with religion.

with an inscription. As may be imagined, these images were offered by young mothers out of gratitude that they could nurse their children. At temples that are visited by many sailors, as for instance the 36th, whose chief divinity is the "Surges-cleaving Fudō", one finds scoops without bottoms, such as it is well-known are kept on almost all Japanese ships, as a protection against disaster at sea. At another temple there were many photographs nailed or pasted up, among them numbers from the United States and Hawaii sent by Japanese emigrants. One also finds frequently in the temples medicine flasks hungs up with the contents, bequeathed by people who have been healed and have no more use for them, as well as crutches and cripples' wagons, given by those who have received the use of their limbs again. At the 44th temple I even discovered a plaster cast, as a sign of the new times and the European art of healing. The outer hall of the 88th temple is literally bristling with crutches, and many people also leave their ticket clamps behind them there. As an indication of the tolerance of Buddhism, it is a significant that at one temple (No.34) I found a practically new large, framed picture of the Virgin Mary. The priest knew very well whom the picture represented. A teacher in the primary school of the place had presented it, and it was a beautiful and good picture. What reception would an image of

Kwannon find in Altotting?[119] The fact that it is not through indifference that there is such broadmindedness is shown by another votive gift that hangs in the 71st temple, the Iyadani-dera in the province of Sanuki. When I saw it, I thought at first that it was another medicine flask, such as I had already seen many of. But this flask was larger, and besides, there seems to be something in it. I asked the priest, who explained to me that this was the little finger of a man who had made a vow at this temple to cut off his finger and send it to the temple, if the wish of his heart should be fulfilled. No doubt it is superstition to wish to serve the divinity in such a way, but one can see from this instance how seriously these people take their belief.[120]

We have already mentioned above the way many straw sandals that are offered to the two Deva Kings at the entrance gate. Many pilgrims make such offerings at the beginning of their pilgrimage, so that they may not receive wounds, or so that their feet may not become weak in any other way. Whoever in the course of the pilgrimage has difficulty in walking also offers a pair of such sandals. Although there are really four Deva Kings, only two are usually placed at the entrance gate. That the sandals are offered especially to them may probably be connected with

---

[119] Altotting is a stronghold of Catholicism (Translator's note)
[120] At the 40th temple there are to be found eight such fingers framed.

the fact that there are two in number. The size is for the most part that of regular foot-gear, but some of double size and even larger are also to be seen everywhere. At some temples, such as the 71st, Iyadani-dera, and the 87th, Nagao-dera, I found sandals that are fully four and a half feet long and correspondingly wide. Naturally, it is only the exception when one finds lacking at a temple the red-lacquered image of Binzuru, who heals the sick.

An unusual thing, which I had never run across until now in Japan, was a little chapel in the Butsumoku-ji (No.42) in southern Iyo, It was called Gyūō-dō, the hall of the Cow King, and stood like a holy shrine upon four posts above three feet high, with double doors opening outwards. Inside there were a larger and (if I remember correctly) two smaller images of cows, besides a chest for offerings, a large rope (probably representing a leading rope), a little candlestick for the reception of sacrificial candles, and some other small articles of worship. On the double doors and over the pillars hung the tickets of many pilgrims, as well as innumerable straw sandals. These sandals, however, were not those of pilgrims, but were the sort that are fastened to the hoofs of cattle. The legend of the founding of this temple relates that Kōbō Daishi on his journey through the mountains met here an old man, who was leading a cow on a cord, and who let the priest, tired from his long walk, ride for a distance. Suddenly they saw something gleaming in a camphor-tree. Kūkai walked nearer to it and saw that it was a jewel that he had thrown into the air before his return from China.[121] Daishi carved a statue of Dainichi Nyorai from the wood of his camphor-tree and placed the jewel upon the forehead between the eyes. Since then, all who seek for the protection and the blessing of the Buddha for their cows or horses come to this temple. Moreover, it possesses many old documents, some of which go back nearly 700 years. That the belief in a protecting power for cattle goes back to a rather far-away past may be seen from the fact that there still exists from the Genroku period a wooden vignette for the printing of charms, which bears the inscription:

Gyūō Butsumoku-ji Hōmyō
(Cow King Buddha Tree Temple Long Life)

Not all temples can boast of such an old tradition. I found also in Tosa at two neighbouring pilgrimage temples, the 35th and the 36th, two ways of driving out sickness, which because of their similarity struck me as remarkable and appeared somewhat suspicious. I could not resist asking a priest whether the custom had existed for a long time, and received the answer that it had already been in existence

---

[121] Compare the legends of the founding of the 36th and the 37th temples on page 150.

earlier, and had been revived about 30 years ago. For the earlier existence there were, however, no documents available, since the part of the temple in which they were kept had been swept away by a spring flood in the Hoei Era (1704-1711). Also, the method of giving notice of it was more reminiscent of a business transaction than of a religious arrangement. A leaflet printed in red with the following words was distributed to all the surrounding villages:

"Hereby be you all informed

On the seventh day of the seventh month of the old calendar from early morning on we shall drive away any and all sickness!! Practice in prayers for exorcising all disease on the day of the Tanabata Festival. Those who attend will please bring one eggplant per person!

Takaoka Community Senryūji

Hereby be you all informed"

In addition to the above notice there was a horizontal board with the following statement:

"These exorcising prayers are held only on the Day of Tanabata."

I myself did not see the preparation for the festival, but I was told that on the appointed day many people with their eggplants made the pilgrimage to the temple, where the priest in his full-dress robes read with his helpers prayers of protection against all sicknesses, and at the end drove these illnesses out into eggplants through exorcism. It need not be said that on that day there was a heavy rain of offerings. The 36th temple held its festival somewhat later on the first or the second day of the Dog, but here the diseases were driven not into eggplants but into cucumbers.

It is well known that, with the exception of the Shin Sect, all the sects sell charms. One can therefore get charms at all 88 temples. Especially beautiful is that of the Ishizuchi Gongen, the incarnation of the highest mountain of Shikoku: an old man, holding in one hand a rolled document, in the other a staff with rings at the top, a feather cloak over his shoulder, *ashida* (high geta) as footgear, sitting upon a kind of stone throne, which runs out above into two falcons' heads, while half-naked Kōbōlds squat at this feet with an axe, an oil flask, and a frame for carrying loads on the back with the swastika on it. The pilgrims like to bring back these charms to relatives and neighbors, and they are to be seen on many house doors. Since I made my pilgrimage just at the time of caring for the summer silkworms, I found at many temples in Awa and Tosa a sign: "*Kaiko no on mamori ga arimasu*" (Charms for silkworms to be had here).

The hōmei juban (life-saving undergarment) and the karamaki on mamori (abdominal-band charm) form another kind of protection against sickness. The first was for sale at Higashidera in Tosa, and was a simple undergarment of white cloth with some seals on it. On the other hand, the abdominal band was, as far as I could see, nothing but white cloth without seals. The charms for an easy birth are also to be had at various temples, although the 61st temple, Kōon-ji, better known by the name of *Koyasu Daishi*, "the child-easy Daishi", holds as it were a monopoly in them.

This temple is a perfect example of how under determined and energetic leadership a temple can reach a high degree of development in a short time. Its history will therefore be discussed here more in detail. About 15 years ago this place of pilgrimage was perhaps the poorest of the 88, but today scarcely one of the other temples can be compared with Kōon-ji, as far as a flourishing condition and prosperity are concerned. The reason is that the present abbot, Suien Yamaoka, has built in the most skillful way upon the foundation of a local legend according to which the Daishi helped a woman of that neighbourhood in childbirth, and left behind at this temple a special, secret charm for childbirth – a cult that has for its central point the Daishi as the helper in all dilemmas concerning children. He founded the Koyasudaishi-kō, i.e., the Community of the Child-easy Daishi; built up gradually a staff of evangelists, who today, eighty in number, travel through the whole countryside, always in groups of three, going even to Korea and into Manchuria, caring for the spiritual unity of the members, whose number runs to about 200,000. Naturally, the temple has also its own devotional sheet, "*Hito to Hotoke*" (Man and Buddha), as one must generally admit that Mr. Yamaoka takes a great interest in being a good shepherd to his people, maintaining as most important the principle that the temple is there not for the priests, but for the believers. Great care therefore is taken at the temple itself for the shelter, the entertainment, and the amusement of the pilgrims, who are all invited to remain, and be sheltered and fed at no expense to themselves. In addition, almost every morning there are lectures for the edification of the pilgrims, and even moving pictures are not lacking. Besides the genuine pilgrims, great numbers of younger and older married couples from all circles of life visit the temple. In the manner and way in which the abbot, a good judge of people, handles them lies perhaps something of the method of Christian Science, as one can see from the text upon which he preaches over and over: "*Tada ichinen bodaishin ni jū sureba subete no kōi ga bodai ni arazaru koto nashi.*"[122]

---

[122] If one lives for only one year in the true devotional spirit, there will be no part of one's conduct that is not spiritual.

234

Several temples claim for themselves an especial protecting power for those in the "dangerous age", basing their claim on the fact that Kūkai stayed at them at the age of 37 or 42 years, and practiced for 37 or 42 days a secret magic for the exorcising of the danger of that particular age. One of the best-known of this kind is the last of the 23 places of pilgrimage of Awa, the Yakuō-ji, at which the Daishi at the age of 42 is said to have applied himself to magic practices. The pamphlet that I received at this temple gives the following instructions for the driving out of danger, called yakuyoke, as well as a brief history of the place:

"The people who are at the age of the Great or the Small danger [123] and wish to turn aside the danger of ill-luck should visit the temple on a favorable day. On their arrival they should first buy a pair of new straw sandals, and when they come to the danger-hill – the men to the men's hill, and the women to the women's hill -, put on these sandals and climb up the stone steps of the danger-hill, the men 42 and women 32, laying upon every step one rin, five rin, or even one sen. In order to drive out the danger to men as well as to women, there is buried under

Translator's note.
[123] The pamphlet specifies as years of the Great Danger for men as 41, 42 and 61; for women 32,33 and 61; as years of the Little Danger for both sexes
1,6,7,15,16,19,24,25,28,34,37,43,46,51,51,55,60,64,69,70,78,79,82.

the men's hill and under the women's hill the Yakushi Sutra copied a thousand times with each character upon a pebble. One must leave the sandals on the top of the hill, and then strike upon the incense jar that is to be found in the *Ema-dō* (Hall of Offerings), but only as many times as there are years in one's true age. Then one must visit all the other buildings of the temple, and at last strike the gong[124] in front of the *Zuigutō*[125] as many times as there are years in one's true age. Then one should offer in the main hall a danger-banishing-lamp and should receive a danger-banishing-charm; and then one should go to the shop and order there danger-banishing prayers."

While here, as can be seen from the buried Yakushi Sutra, the relation to the Daishi is more historical, and the real helper-in-need is the great healer of disease, Yakushi, there are in other places in Shikoku and in other parts of Japan statues of the Daishi there are called Yaku-yoke-Daishi. Toyoshiro Takeda has searched through the newspaper, Mikkyō, to find out the extent of the existence of such danger-banishing-statues of other persons and divinities, and has come to the conclusion that the Yaku-

---

[124] Japanese: keiban or kei; see illustration in Brinkley.
[125] Zuiutō signifies really the temple (or chapel) of Daizuigu Bosatsu (Mahaapratisaraa), who is called in the Mikkyō "Yog-wan Kongō" (the Listening-to-prayer Diamond), because he surely grants prayers. Apparently under this chapel there are also buried characters of the Daizuigu Darani-Sutra written on stone.

yoke-Daishi are more numerous than all other statues taken together. With the exception of the Daishi-statues, those of Kwannon, Jizō, and Yakushi are the most numerous. Many of these statues are ascribed to the Daishi himself, but Crown Prince Shōtoku and Nichiren Shōnin are likewise said to have carved and set up such exorcising images. Of the Yakuyoke-Daishi, however, none is set up in a pilgrimage temple as the chief divinity, although the 20th temple possesses such a statue.

The best known are between the 53rd and the 54th temples in the Henjōin at Kikuma, a temple which as *bangai fudasho* (a ticket-place lying outside the round) is visited by a great many pilgrims, and in the Konkōzan (or Kindōzan) Senryū-ji, the holy of holies of the 65th pilgrimage temple. In both temples today Kōbō Daishi is the chief divinity, but I can assert, at least of the Henjōin, that originally Yakushi Nyorai was reverenced there. One can thus see how the figure of the Daishi is able to replace even other divinities. Takeda designates this reverence of the Daishi in guise of a protector against danger as the highest manifestation of the Japanese popular faith, as far as it concerns the Daishi. According to my opinion, the significance of the Daishi in the popular faith of the Japanese is not exhausted by the above explanation. Above all, however, I should like to see in it an important start on the development of the figure of the Daishi into that of a religious mediator, as discussed in the next chapter.

Conclusion: Summary
Shingon as a Religion of Salvation by Faith
(*Tariki Shūkyō*)

We come to the conclusion. In the previous chapters an attempt was made to give the reader a description of the phenomenon of the Shikoku pilgrimage. We briefly traced the origin of the custom of making pilgrimages, beginning with the spiritual founder; then studied the four provinces and their temples; and at last turned to the pilgrim, his equipment and his customs, walked with him in front of the halls of the temples, and searched with him for his simple inns. While doing this, the details of the picture were gradually filled in and the whole has finally attained, we hope, a certain clarity and vividness. But there may be some who will ask wherein really lies the special significance of the Shikoku pilgrimage, the point in which it is different from other pilgrimages. Is it only the circumstances that the pilgrims are more numerous on the Four-Province-Island than on other pilgrim roads? In other words; might one say that it is only a difference of degree that distinguishes the 88 temples in their significance as places of pilgrimage, or is there to be discovered something more than that, something special, something materially different?

First, it is well known that entirely aside from the

religious element every pilgrimage has an education significance of the people. It was probably still greater in earlier times, when the people were not yet able to travel so easily and so much as today. But even in the present it is not unimportant, when every year thousands and tens of thousands leave their homes and journey as pilgrims through a section of their fatherland that they would never in their lives have visited under other circumstances, and even in later years will probably not visit again. How many memories they bring home with them! How their feeling of belonging together as fellow-countrymen is strengthened when they travel along with pilgrims from other provinces! How many come for the first time to the realization that behind the mountains also dwell people! As far as this significance of the pilgrimage is concerned, the 88 temples are of comparatively little importance, but just here we must constantly keep in mind a particular point, which we touched upon briefly at the beginning and discussed in detail in the chapter on settai: never do the pilgrims find anything approaching such a great sympathy on the part of the inhabitants of the region of any pilgrimage as just here in Shikoku. The educational significance is therefore not confined to the pilgrim, but extends as well to the inhabitants of the four provinces which they pass.[126]

---

[126] How highly the educational significance of the pilgrimage is

The custom of going on pilgrimage is also not without economic significance. Without doubt it brings to the pilgrim in most cases an improvement in health that is afterwards noticeable economically in an increased capacity for work. As for the special economic significance for Shikoku, however, someone has said that the introduction of the pilgrimage has been the most beautiful legacy that the Daishi could have made to his native place, for in this way every year hundreds of thousands of yen come into the island. As we have seen, almost every pilgrim takes with him as the cost of his journey from thirty to sixty yen, and in many cases even more. If we assume that of the 30,000 people who travel through Shikoku each year only a third come from outside – the number is probably much larger -, we have the neat sum of from 300,000 to 600,000 yen brought into the island by the pilgrims. In addition, there are individual temple, e.g., the 54th and the 61st, which received monetary aid from all over the country. There are also considerable sums coming into Shikoku from outside sources for the purposed of erecting new buildings. For instance, at the rebuilding of the 64th temple,

---

prized by the Japanese is shown in the joint publication by the agricultural associations of the four provinces of Shikoku (Matsuyama, September 1929) of an "Agricultural Guide along the road of the Shikoku pilgrimage." In this department especially Shikoku shows rarities even for Japanese, besides a great number of associated enterprises, which are excellently carried on and at which the 242-page guidebook likewise hints.

the stone entrance came from Okayama, the stone flagstones leading to the two main halls from the province of Bitchū, the lumber from a rich merchant in Osaka, and so forth. One might therefore say that the stream of blessings that spreads every year over Shikoku flows back again only in part through *settai*, if it were not true that those who dispense the settai do not as a rule belong in the company of those who are the direct recipients of the golden blessing.

As for the significance of the pilgrimage in a religious sense, there is here too a difference of degree to be established with respect to other pilgrimages, while it can be said that the Shikoku pilgrimage, by virtue of the great number of pilgrims who undertake it yearly, has a prominent part in raising the standard of and strengthening popular piety. For many the pilgrimage, to whatever temples it may be, is and remains the greatest religious experience of their days, and this especially the case in Shikoku, where the factors of fashion and pleasure can be said with truth to be wholly set aside. For that very reason, however, the Shikoku pilgrimage exhibits a phenomenon that distinguishes it from all other pilgrimages. Aside from the question that Tomita raises, as to whether the mountain-top Buddhism has not been preserved in the purest form in Shikoku, the phenomemon that in our opinion lends a special feeling to the 88 holy places is the remarkable fact that Kōbō Daishi becomes for the average pilgrim more and more a kind of mediator, through whose grace he finds the way to Nirvana. Shingon – not the official dogmatism, but the general popular belief – thus undergoes a change of which Kōbō Daishi would never have allowed himself to dream. We shall search in vain through all the many writings of the Daishi for a word such as it reported to have come down from Jesus, "No man cometh to the Father, but through me," and yet, it is the case today that "Daishi no go riyaku" (the grace of the Daishi) and "Namu Daishi Henjō Kongō" (I rely on the Daishi, the Lighting-all, the Diamond) play a role not only the pilgrim-road, but also far beyond it, that closely approaches that of the Saviour of the Christian Church. Possible this development came about through the fact that Kōbō Daishi is looked upon as an incarnation of Vairocana, but the greatest factor in bringing about such a condition has been the Shikoku Pilgrimage, and it is remarkable that Vairocana has retreated so entirely into the background – at least, as far as the popular faith is concerned. Is it only the need of the people for a concrete form, which has fixed itself in this case on the towering personality of the Daishi, or does the belief in Amida exert an unconscious influence here? Those are questions whose solution will come through special studies, and perhaps even then only partially, but which appear to be worthy of further research. Elements in the development, as already noted above, are to be seen in the Yakuyoke-statues as well as in the special significance that the pilgrim staff has gradually acquired on the Shikoku pilgrimage. In every case we are faced with the fact that in this way Shingon, contrary to its original nature, has become a religion of salvation by faith (tariki shūkyō) for wide circles of people, and, as the following paragraphs will show, not for laymen only.

We close this discussion with the re-printing of an essay, "My Rebirth", which appeared in 1921 in a little book, *Shikoku Reijō,* and can serve as a good illustration of what has been said above about the pilgrimage as a religious experience. At the same time, however, since the author appears to be a priest, it shows that the development of Shingon into a religion of salvation by faith is not confined to the laity.

My Rebirth

By Shōsei Kobayashi

Director of the Inkōsha, Tokyo

"If I am to speak about my spiritual condition at the time that I undertook my pilgrimage in the 40th year of the Meiji Era (1907) at the age of 32 years, I must first remark that at that time I had had various sorrows and wanted to overcome these through the pilgrimage. To write more in detail would require a whole volume of poetry, but I will name two or three reasons. First, I had had the misfortune to fall in love; experiencing the sorrow of love in the spring of life is a frequent occurrence. In the second place, doubt had laid held of me. How did it happen that people were not at honest in dealing with me, even though I was honest in dealing with them? Why should I be troubled with doubts at all, although they were all honest doubts? Such doubts as these, and others, gave me endless trouble and tormented me. In the third place, my failure with my students, the insufficiency of my education, harassed me, so that I could not teach the students properly, and so brought failure to both them and myself. In the fourth place, I was grieving because of the death of my mother. And so forth, and so forth, for I could go on for some time yet. In brief, I was a child of sorrow, felt myself a prisoner to grief, and now hoped to lose this grief through the person of the Daishi and through my own comprehensive experience. I wanted to taste the feeling of freedom, and if I did not succeed, I thought I might as well die. So I made the great decision and set out on the journey. At that time I was without doubt suffering from a nervous breakdown. Whatever others did or said went to my heart, without by being able to do anything about it, and if I could not put an end to this condition, I thought that it would be better to die. My mood at that time was like someone wanting to pierce a sheet of iron with this bare fist.

"I therefore set out upon the pilgrimage and travelled through Iyo and then Tosa without noticing any special change. But in Tosa a psychological and physiological change took place in me. I became conscious of how feeble my strength was, how many my faults, how utterly weak I myself was, and this feeling became stronger and stronger within me. After I had returned home also, this change, psychological as well as physiological, became stronger and stronger within me.

Eyesight:
Figures of Buddha of all sizes swim before my eyes.

Hearing:
I hear far-away music in the dead of night.

Taste:

Pickles and such things suddenly taste sweet to me.

Feelings:

I have a feeling as though blood were flowing out of my bosom.

Memory:

I feel as though it has grown extremely strong.

"I wondered whether I had not become mad, and thought that I was attacked by a zenma (Zen-devil). I read the 'Zenbamonmistu Jidai Hōmon' of Chisha Daishi[127], and I became more and more certain that I was suffering from the Zen-illness.[128] I exerted myself strenuously in order to bring my spirit back to a normal condition. When I think back today and see how I was following only my own enlightenment without a guide, it appears to me to have

---

[127] Chisha Daishi is a Chinese priest, the founder of the Tendai sect. I could not find the work mentioned in the Bukkyō Daijiten; perhaps there is a misprint (Zenbaramitsu instead of Zen-bamonmitsu)

[128] Zen-illness (zenbyō) is, according to the Bukkyō Daijiten, a Buddhist designation for mental aberration, which is laid to possession by spirits. I believe, however, - in agreement with numerous Japanese whom I have questioned about the matter – that the word zenbyō means here a madness brought on through the Dhyana (in Japanese: zen).

been a great danger, but it seems that I found Life in the midst of Death. Finally, I felt that I was normal again, and since then my body, aside from colds that I catch through carelessness, has been healthy, my spirit keen, my tenth-rate short-sightedness has almost completely left me, and a disease of the nose from which I suffered is entirely healed. My strength of feeling (ability to receive impressions?) has increased; I have a desire to paint, although in former times I never gave a thought as to how an artist went about painting a picture; and the range and carrying ability of my voice are increasing daily. Yes, I feel as though newly-born through the grace of the Daishi. Now I think of what a miserable creature I was formerly, without consciousness, like a grain of wheat, and on the basis of my advance in belief I urge others to undertake the pilgrimage, which I have made twice more despite my age. My students too have gone, and my friends.

But whoever goes upon the pilgrimage must

First: be without any strong desires.

Second: believe absolutely

Third: Persevere in effort.

"Upon the one who gives heed to these three important points and has only the Daishi in his heart will the Daishi himself shed his wonderful radiance

"Namu Daishi Henjō Kongō!"

Supplement

A. A List of the 88 Temples

General Remarks

In the guidebooks of the present day the temples in general are designated by only two names: 1) the so-called "Mountain Name", usually but not always ending in –san (-zan) = mountain[129], and so hinting at the Chinese mountain temples, which were originally the mother-cloisters of the Japanese holy places; and 2) the real temple name, usually ending in –ji and less often in –tera (-dera). The older sources give us in addition still a third name ending in -in[130] The images[131] of the chief deities that are designated as national treasures are indicated by a (!). In addition to these, however, there are a great number of buildings, image, and other art treasures that are likewise national treasures. Variations of the present names from those given in older sources are found in 21 cases, but

---

[129] In regard to the pronunciation of san: the guidebooks *Shikoku Henro Dōgyō Futari* and *Shikoku Reijō Reisan*, which are consulted about the names, give with few exceptions the voice pronunciation –zan for three-quarters of all the names; for only one-quarter have both guidebooks –san, which in these cases comes after a short vowel, or from the ei, or sometimes you, which was originally in the Chinese ing (Nos.7,8, 65)

[130] in= office, school, building for religious purposes; used commonly today by mission schools (e.g., Meiji Gakuin, Kwansai Gakuin, etc)

[131] In the case of Temple No.68 a painted picture is referred to.

these are mostly concerned with variations in writing, in such cases as they have not been removed to be shiftings due to the separation of Buddhism and Shintoism after the Restoration (Temples No.13,30,etc). It is nevertheless interesting that the mountain name, Ishizuchizan, of Temple No.60, identical with that of Temple No.64, is of a later date, for in the old guidebooks it is called Bukkōzan (like No.75). The reading is that given in the guidebooks of today, although according to Buddhist usage one or the other characters ought to be read differently.

No.	Mountain Name	Temple Name	Chief Deity	Founder
1	Chikuwasan	Reisan-ji (Ryōsen-ji)	Shaka Nyorai	Gyōgi Bosatsu
2	Nisshōwan	Gokuraku-ji	Amida Nyorai	Gyōgi Bosatsu
3	Kin(w)ōzan	Konsen-ji	Shaka Nyorai	Gyōgi Bosatsu
4	Kokuganzan	Dainichi-ji	Dainichiji Nyorai	(Not named)
5	Mujinzan	Jizō-ji	Shōgun Jizō Bosatsu	Kōbō Daishi
6	Onsenzan	Anraku-ji	Yakushi Nyorai	Kōbō Daishi
7	K(w)ō myō-san	Jūraku-ji	Amida Nyorai	Kōbō Daishi
8	Fumyousan	Kurodan-ji	1000-handed Kwannon	Kōbō Daishi
9	Shō kakuzan	Hōrin-ji	Nehan no ShakaNyorai	Kōbō Daishi
10	Tokudosan	Kirihata-ji	1000-handed Kwannon	Kōbō Daishi
11	Kongōzan	Fujizen-ji	Yakushi Nyorai	Kōbō Daishi
12	Marosan	Shōsan-ji	Kokūzō Bosatsu	En no Gyōja
13	Ogurizan	Dainichi-ji	11-faced Bosatsu	not specified
14	Seijuzan	Jōraku-ji	Miroku Bosatsu	Kōbō Daishi
15	Yakuouzan	Kokubun-ji	Yakushi Nyorai	ordered by Emperor Shōmu
16	K(w)ōkizan	Kwannon-ji	1000-handed Kwannon	Kōbō Daishi
17	Rurisan	Myōshō-ji (Idoji)	Yakushi Nyorai	Shōtoku Taishi

18	Boyōzan	Onsan-ji	Yakushi Nyorai	Gyōgi Bosatsu
19	Ma-nisan	Tatsue-ji (Tachieji)	Jizō Bosatsu	Gyōgi Bosatsu at the order of Emperor Shōmu
20	Reishūzan	Kakurin-ji	Shōgun Jizō Bosatsu	Kōbō Daishi
21	Shashinzan	Dairyū-ji	Kokūzō Bosatsu	Kōbō Daishi
22	Makusuizan	Byōdō-ji	Yakushi Nyorai	Kōbō Daishi
23	I(w)ōzan	Yakuō-ji	Yakushi Nyorai	Gyōgi Bosatsu
24	Murotozan	Saimisaki-ji (Higashid-era)	Kokūzō Bosatsu	Kōbō Daishi
25	Hōjuzan	Tsushō-ji (Tsudera)	Jizō Bosatsu	Kōbō Daishi
26	Ryūtōzan	Kongōchō-ji (Nishidera)	Yakushi Nyorai	Kōbō Daishi
27	Chikurinzan	Kōnomine-ji	11-faced Kwannon	Gyōgi Bosatsu at the order of Emperor Shōmu
28	Hōkaizan	Dainichi-ji	Dainichi Nyorai	Gyōgi Bosatsu
29	Ma-nisan	Kokubun-ji	1000-handed Kwannon	Gyōgi Bosatsu
30	Momoyama	Anraku-ji	Amida Nyorai	not specified
31	Godaisan	Chikurin-ji	Monju Bosatsu	Gyōgi Bosatsu

254

32	Hachiyōzan	Zenjihō-ji (Minedera)	11-faced Kwannon	Gyōgi Bosatsu
33	Kōfukuzan	Sekkei-ji	Yakushi Nyorai	Kōbō Daishi
34	Motōsan	Tanema-ji	Yakushi Nyorai	Shotoku Taishi
35	I(w)ōzan	Kiyotaki-ji	Yakushi Nyorai	Gyōgi Bosatsu
36	Dokkosan	Seiryu-ji	Namikiri Fudō Myōō	Kōbō Daishi
37	Fujiisan	Iwamoto-ji	Amida Nyorai	not specified
38	Ashizurizan	Kongō-fuku-ji	1000-handed Kwannon	Kōbō Daishi
39	Terayama	Enk(w)ō-ji	Ansan Yakushi Nyorai	Gyōgi Bosatsu at the order of Emperor Shō mu
40	Heijōzan	Kwanjizai-ji	Yakushi Nyorai	Kōbō Daishi
41	Inariyama (Inarisan)	Ryūk(w)ū-ji	11-faced Kwannon	Kōbō Daishi
42	Ikkwazan	Butsu-moku-ji	Dainichi Nyorai	Kōbō Daishi
43	Genk(w)ōzan	Akeshi-ji	1000-faced Kwannon	Kōbō Daishi
44	Sugō zan	Daihō-ji	11-faced Kwannon	At the order of Emperor Monbu
45	Kaiganzan	Iwaya-ji	Fudō Myōō	Kōbō Daishi
46	I(w)ōzan	Jōruri-ji	Yakushi Nyorai	Gyōgi Bosatsu

47	Kumanosan	Yasaka-dera	Amida Nyorai	En no Gyoja
48	Kiyotakizan	Sairin-ji	11-faced Kwannon	Gyōgi Bosatsu
49	Sairinzan	Jōdo-ji	Shaka Nyorai	Gyōgi Bosatsu
50	Higashi-yama	Hanta-ji	Yakushi Nyorai	Gyōgi Bosatsu
51	Kumanosan	Ishite-ji	Yakushi Nyorai	Gyōgi Bosatsu
52	Ryūnzan	Taisan-ji	11-faced Kwannon	Gyōgi Bosatsu at the order of Emperor Shō mu
53	Tsugasan	Enmyō-ji	Amida Nyorai	Gyōgi Bosatsu
54	Kinkenzan	Enmei-ji (Enmyō-ji) [1]	Fudō Myōō	Gyōgi Bosatsu
55	Betsugū	Nankōbō	DaiTsūshō Butsu [2]	Transferred from Ōmishima during the reign of the Emperor Mombu
56	Konrinzan	Taisan-ji	Jizō Bosatsu	Kōbō Daishi at the order of Emperor Yōmei
57	Futōzan	Eifuku-ji	Amida Nyorai	not specified

58	Sareizan	Senyū-ji	1000-handed Kwannon	At the order of Emperor Tenchi
59	Kink(w)ōzan	Kokubun-ji	Yakushi Nyorai	Gyōgi Bosatsu
60	Ishitetsuzan	Yokomine-ji	Dainichi Nyorai	not specified
61	Sendanzan	Kōon-ji (Koyasu Daishi)	Dainichi Nyorai	Shotoku Taishi
62	Ichinomiya	Hōju-ji	11-faced Kwannon	at the order of Emperor Shōmu
63	Mikkyōzan	Kisshō-ji	Bishamonten	not specified
64	Ishitetsuzan	Maegami-ji	Amida Nyorai	not specified
65	Yūreizan	Sankaku-ji	11-faced Kwannon	Gyōgi Bosatsu
66	Kyobetsusan	Unpen-ji	1000-handed Kwannon	Kōbō Daishi at the order of Emperor Saga
67	Koma-tsu(w)osan	Daikō-ji	Yakushi Nyorai	Kōbō Daishi
68	Kotohikizan	Hachiman-gū	Raikō no Amida Nyorai	Nisshō Jōnin, a saint of the Hossō Sect
69	Shichihō zan	Kwannon-ji	Shō-Kwannon	Kōbō Daishi

70	Shichihō zan	Moto-yama-ji	Batō-Myōō	Kōbō Daishi
71	Kengozan	Iyadana-ji	1000-handed Kwannon	Gyōgi Bosatsu
72	Gahaishizan	Mandara-ji	Dainichi Nyorai	(not specified; temple where Kūkai's ancestors are buried)
73	Gahaishizan	Shussaka-ji	Yakushi Nyorai	Kōbō Daishi
74	I(w)ōzan	Kōyama-ji [3]	Yakushi Nyorai	not specified
75	Byōbu-ga-Ura	Zentsū-ji	Yakushi Nyorai	Kōbō Daishi's birthplace
76	Keisokuzan	Konzō-ji	Yakushi Nyorai	Wake no Dōzen Chōjin
77	Kuwatasan [4]	Dōryū-ji	Yakushi Nyorai	Prince Wake no Dōryū
78	Bukk(w)ōzan	Gōshō-ji	Amida Nyorai	Gyōgi Bosatsu
79	Kinkwazan	Kōshō-in	11-faced Kwannon	Kōbō Daishi

80	Maku-gyūzan	Kokubun-ji	1000-handed Kwannon	not specified; probably Gyōgi Bosatsu at the order of Emperor Shōmu
81	Ayastasan	Shiramine-ji	1000-handed Kwannon	Kōbō and Chishō Daishi
82	Seihō zan	Negoro-ji	1000-handed Kwannon	Kōbō and Chishō Daishi
83	Shinmōsan	Ichinomiya	Sei-Kwannon	During the reign of the Emperor Monbu Kanshin
84	Nammenzan	Yashima-ji	1000-handed Kwannon	The Chinese abbot Kanshin (Chien Chen)
85	Gokenzan	Yakuri-ji	Sei-Kannon	Kōbō Daishi
86	Fudaraku-zan	Shido-ji	11-faced Kwannon	The nun Sonoko, a reincarnation of Monju Bosatsu
87	Fudaraku-zan	Naga(w)o-dera	Sei-Kwannon	Gyōgi Bosatsu

88	I(w)ōzan	Ōkubo-ji	Yakushi Nyorai	Gyōgi Bosatsu

1. Translator's Note – 1st reading given in a pilgrim guidebook; 2nd reading given in list

2. Translator's Note: In a pilgrim guidebook, it is "DaiTsū-chishō Butsu

3. Translator's Note: In a pilgrim guidebook, "Kosanji"

4. Translator's Note: In a pilgrim guidebook, "Sōtasan"

260

B. <u>A List of expressions and phrases referring to the pilgrimage or that are used frequently by the pilgrims.</u>[1]

The following list makes no pretence of being complete, but is confined chiefly to summing up the expressions that occur in the book, for the sake of convenience in referring to them. There is a great need for a thorough study of the speech of pilgrims from a Japanese pen.

Ajirogasa (網代笠)– a hat made of thin, plaited bamboo; the pilgrim hat of earlier times.

Amagu (雨具)– literally, "rain article", usually a piece of oil-paper or a round cloak (*kappa*) of the same material; in earlier times, also a rush mat (see under *goza*)

Ashinaka (足中), Ashinaka zōri （足中草履） – straw sandals that afford protection to the sole of the foot only, leaving the heal free; no longer used today, only a miniature pair being still carried as footgear for the Daishi.

Bangai (番外)– a place of worship lying outside of the succession of the 88 temples, but that is nevertheless visited by a majority of pilgrims, and also gives a seal; several of the bangai are of proved ancient origin, but there are many new and doubtful ones.

Byōkioroshi (病気下ろし) – literally, "a letting-down of

---

[1] Editor – Bohner did not include the Japanese characters in the original, but Merrill added them to the English translation. However, some of the characters she wrote are no longer used, so I have written them in their modern style.

sickness", a pilgrimage made for the purpose of obtaining the healing of disease.

Chōzu (手水) – water for washing

Chōzubachi (手水鉢) – basin with water for washing the hands

Daisan (代参) – a pilgrimage by proxy.

Daishi (大師)– Kōbō Daishi, the founder of Shingon in Japan.

Daishi no ana (大師の穴) – "Daishi holes", the term used in the southern part of Tosa for the holes of the charcoal piles.

Daishidō (大師堂) – the Daishi-hall of the temple of pilgrimage.

Daishi no on hakiyō (大師の御履料) – "the footgear of the Daishi" (see ashinaka)

Daishi no hōgō (大師の法号)– "the jewel-name of the Daishi" the name received upon his consecration as the Patriarch of Shingon, "Henjō Kongō."

Daishi no kajimizu (大師の火事水) – springs founds in several places on the pilgrimage, and said to have been caused to gush forth by prayers of incantation (kajikitō) offered by the Daishi.

Daishi no go yō (大師の御用)– "necessary supplies for the Daishi", a tiny imitation of a straw sack, taken along as baggage for the Daishi (see nidawara).

Daishi mo fude no ayamari (大師も筆の誤り)– "Even the Daishi makes a mistake with his brush at times." = to err is human.

262

Ishi wa Daishi no atama nari: nemutte mo fumubekarazu (石は大師の頭なり、眠っても踏むべからず)– "Stones are the head of the Daishi; even in sleep one should not step on them." (A warning to the pilgrims to spare their feet.)

Kōya Daishi (高野大師)– The Kōya Daishi, the best-known picture of the Daishi; who is portrayed sitting upon a priest's chair.

Koyasu Daishi (子安大師)– "The Child-easy Daishi", a statue of the Daishi in Kōon-ji (No.61) with a child, known far and wide as of marvelous potency.

Taiko wa Hideyoshi ni torare, Daishi wa Kōbō ni torareru (太閤は秀吉に取られ、大師は弘法に取られる)– "Hideyoshi has made himself the embodiment of the title Taiko, and Daishi of the title Kōbō." A proverb demonstrating the fame of Kōbō Daishi.

Yakuyoke Daishi (厄除け大師)– Statues of the Daishi that possess the power to exorcise the danger of certain ages.

Dōgyō (同行)– fellow-travellers

Dōgyō futari (同行二人)– "two fellow-travellers", the inscription on the ticket, the staff, etc. of the pilgrim to signify that the pilgrimage is being made together with Kōbō Daishi.[2]

Eika (詠歌), go eika (御詠歌)– hymns of the temples

Ema-dō (絵馬堂)– the place of votive offerings of the temple; the hall in which the votive pictures hang.

Fuda (札), o-fuda (御札)– a ticket offered by the pilgrim at every temple and on certain other occasions.

---

[2] Editor – The correct reading is "dōgyō ninin."

Fudabasami (札鋏)– ticket-clamps, - two little boards between which the pilgrim keeps his tickets.

Fudanagashi (札流し)– "letting the tickets float away," a yearly festival at Takahama near Matsuyama, at which all the tickets for one year from the ten temples in the former domains of Matsuyama (No.44-53) are given to the sea.

Fudasho (札所)– a temple at which the ticket is presented, i.e., a temple of the pilgrimage.

Fuda wo osameru　(札を納める)– to present a ticket

Fuda wo utsu (札を打つ)– "to nail a ticket", i.e. to hang it up at a temple.

Goma (護摩), gomashugyō (護摩修行)– one of the most important practices of the secret teaching of Shingon – a kind of fire-mass, at which sutras are read during the burning of wood, foliage, and incense before the picture of the deity.

Gomadan (護摩壇)– the goma-altar, the place where the goma is held.

Gomaden (護摩殿)– the goma-hall; a special hall for the goma, found in a few temples, such as No. 61.

Gomazu (護摩酢)– goma-vinegar, a euphemistic designation for wine, which is forbidden to the pilgrim.

Gomen no Watashi (御免の渡し)– "The Crossing of the Illustrious Permission"; a place on the pilgrimage where, according to legend, Kōbō Daishi has permitted the pilgrim to travel for a distance by boat.

Goza (茣蓙)– rush matting, generally used in earlier times by pilgrims as a protection against rain and wind; still carried today in Shikoku only by those making a pilgrimage to Mount Tsurugi.

Gyaku (逆), junpai wo gyaku ni suru (巡拝を逆にする)– to make a pilgrimage in reverse order.

Hakui no kimono (白衣の着物)– the white attire of the pilgrim.

Hendo (遍ど)– a variation of henro in country dialect

Henjō Kongō (遍照金剛)– "the All-brightening, the Diamond", the name given to Kōbō Daishi at the time of his consecration as the Patriarch of Shingon

Henrei (遍礼)– a pilgrimage

Henro (遍路)– originally, a pilgrimage; today, the designation for a pilgrim.

Henro no dōgu (遍路の道具)– the equipment of a pilgrim.

Henro no fukusō (遍路の服装)– the pilgrim attire.

Henrogu (遍路具)= henro no dōgu (遍路の道具)

Henro no mi, henro no budō (遍路の實、遍路の葡萄)– "pilgrim fruits", "pilgrim grape berries" – a popular term for certain edible wild berries.

Henromichi (遍路道)– a pilgrim road

Henro no sekisho (遍路の関所)– temple that are noted for the heavenly chastisement experienced at them by unrepentant pilgrims. No.12 and 40 are regarded of especial worth as sekisho.

Hondō (本堂)– the chief hall of the temple.

Hōnō suru (奉納する)– the Chinese reading of *osametatematsuru*; to make an offering , to consecrate.

Honzon (本尊), go honzon (御本尊)– the chief deity of a

temple.

Hora (法螺)– a conch shell often called hōra; in order to liken the first syllable to hō, the Buddhist teaching.

Hōtō (宝塔)– the two-storey treasure pagoda of a temple.

Inge (院家)– a polite designation for the abbot of the temple.

Ingen (隠元), ingensama (隠元様)– a frequent form of the above in the speech of the people.

Ishi wa Daishi no atama (石は大師の頭)– see Daishi, above.

Izariguruma (居行車)– A cart used by lame pilgrims.

Jōshūsha (常習者)– "a creature of habit", one who makes a business of going on pilgrimage.

Jun (巡): henro wo jun ni suru (遍礼を巡にする)– to make a pilgrimage in the proper order.

Jun (巡): Anata wa jun desu ka. Gyaku desu ka. (あなたは巡ですか。逆ですか)– "Are you making the

pilgrimage in the proper order or in the reverse order?

Junpai (巡拝)– a pilgrimage

Junpaisha (巡拝者)– a pilgrim

Junrei (巡礼)– a pilgrimage

Jūshoku (住職)– the abbot or head priest of a temple.

Juzu (数珠)– a rosary

Kaichō (開帳), go kaichō (御開帳)– the ceremonial unveiling of a picture (or an image) of Buddha.

Kaiki (開基)– the founding of a temple.

Kaisan (開山)– the founding of a temple, especially with reference to a temple in the mountain.

Kajikitō (加持祈祷)– incantations.

Kajimizu (加持水)– springs that have been caused to flow by incantations.

Kakezure (掛け連れ)– "hangers-on", wayside companions who attach themselves to someone on the journey, often with an intend to defraud.

Kanetsukidō (鐘撞堂)– a bell-tower

Kasa (笠)– a brief designation for the pilgrim hat.

Katajikenaku (忝く)– "most gratefully", the usual form of thanks returned by the pilgrims when receiving gifts.

Kongōzue (金剛杖)– "the diamond staff", the pilgrim staff.

Kōya Daishi　(高野大師)– see Daishi, above.

Koyasu Daishi (子安大師)– see Daishi, above.

Kuwazu imo (食わず芋)– one of the plants resembling the *satoimo* (Colocasia antiquorum) whose tubers are, according to legend, inedible because of the curse of the Daishi. The probability is that it is a poisonous variety native to the tropics, since it appears at Cape Muroto.

Kuwazu kai (食わず貝)– "inedible shellfish", petrified shellfish that are found at an altitude of over 1000 feet at the 27th temple, and that according to the legend were turned to stone by a curse of the Daishi.

Kuwazu nashi (食わず梨)– "inedible pears" at the 84th temple; explanation similar to the preceding.

Kyahan (脚袢)– leggings.

Kyō (経)– a sutra.

Kyōkatabira (経帷子)– the white pilgrim costume.

Kyōzō (経蔵)– "a sutra storehouse", a six-sided building for the preservation of the sutras.

Mairi (詣)– a pilgrimage.

O mairi (お詣り); Yō o mairi de gozaimasu (ようお詣りでございます)– the usual greetings between pilgrims; something like, "A good pilgrimage to you!"

Mairimichi (詣道)– a pilgrim road.

Mamori (守り), on mamori (御守り)– amulets or charms.

Mawaru (廻る)– "to travel around", to go on pilgrimage.

Meguru (廻る)– the same as the above.

O meguri (お廻り)– a pilgrimage.

Mentsū (面桶)– a little box hung from a cord around the neck and carried in front for the receipt of gifts; used infrequently nowadays.

Mōde (詣で)– a visit to a temple.

Mōderu (詣でる)– to visit a temple.

"Namu Daishi Henjō Kongō" (南無大師遍照金剛)– "I trust in the Daishi, the All-illuminating, the Diamond"; the pilgrims' prayer, used also as a greeting or as thanks during the practice of shugyō.

"Nama daikon hendo ni kuwase" (生大根遍どに食わせ)– "Give the pilgrim a raw radish to eat"; a facetious distortion of the above. Often said to pilgrims by children as a comment on their good appetites.

Nidai (荷臺)– a portable frame for luggage.

Nidawara (荷俵)– a bag for the luggage; originally, an ordinary straw sack for the reception of things carried on the journey. A tiny imitation is carried even today as the "Daishi no go yō."

Nidora (荷どら)– a variation of the above in the language of

268

the people.

Nigōri (荷行李)– a basket for luggage.

Nōkyō (納経)– a written offering; formerly, the offering of the whole or a part of a sutra, for which a money payment is substituted today.

Nōkyōchō (納経帳)– the register for the written offerings; the book in which the pilgrim keeps a record of his visit to every temple, and in which he has the temple seals stamped.

Nōkyōhon (納経本)– the book for the offerings of writings; another designation for the preceding.

Nokyōkaki (納経書き)– "the writer of the written offerings"; the person who makes the entries in the *nōkyōchō*.

Nokyōsho (納経所)– the place for written offerings; the window at which the writing is done.

Nōsatsu (納札)– the Chinese reading for fuda.

Nōsatsu suru (納札する)– to give up one's ticket.

Nyonin kinsei (女人禁制)– "forbidden to women"; women are forbidden to tread in certain holy places, but today the enforcement of this ordinance is found in very few places.

Oidai (負臺)= nidai (荷臺).

Oizuri (負笈)– a small portable shrine with a hat fastened above it.

Okunoin (奥の院)– "the innermost temple", a temple that generally lies much deeper in the mountains than the temples of the pilgrimage. Such a temple might also be designated as the "most holy" of the temples of the pilgrimage.

Osameru (納める)– to consecrate.

Osametatematsuru (納め奉る)– the same word as above, but in a more polite form.

Reimairi (礼参り), on reimairi (御礼参り)– a pilgrimage of thanks; a repetition of the pilgrimage in gratitude for the fulfillment of a prayer

Reimawarai (礼廻り), On reimawari (御礼廻り)– "the round of gratitude"; the same as the above

Rei (霊)– "holy", when used in compounds

Reiboku (霊木)– a holy tree.

Reijō (霊場)– "holy places", a designation of the temples of the pilgrimage.

Reiken (霊験)– a holy sign, a holy agency, marvelous power.

Reisatsu (霊刹)– a holy temple, especially a temple with marvelous powers.

Reisen (霊泉)– a holy spring of water, a spring with marvelous powers.

Rin (鈴)– the bell of the pilgrim.

Riyaku (利益), go-riyaku (御利益)– the grace, or the blessing, of the Daishi.

Ryōbu Shintō (両部神道)– "two-fold Shinto", the teaching of the Shingon Sect, according to which the *kami* and the *hotoke* are identical.

Saikō (再興)– the founding anew of an ancient temple that had fallen into ruins.

San-ebukuro (さん絵袋), sanya (さんや)– a pocket hung about the neck in which to receive gifts; used nowadays mostly by priests.

Sangakubukkyō　(山岳仏教)– mountain-top Buddhism.

Sanya (さんや), san-ebukuro (さん絵袋)

Sekisho (関所)– see henro, above.

Senkō (線香)– incense.

Settai (接待)– volunteer entertainment and service of all kinds that are given to pilgrims by the local inhabitants.

Settaibune (接待舟)– boats that come in the spring from Kyushu and Wakayama to Shikoku with gifts for the pilgrims.

Shakujō (錫杖)– a large pilgrim staff with metal rings at the top.

O Shikoku (お四国)– the Shikoku pilgrimage.

O Shikokusama (お四国様)– the Shikoku pilgrimage.

O Shikokumeguri　(お四国廻り)– the Shikoku pilgrimage.

Shingan (心願)– One's heart's desire, and also the vows undertaken to gain this desire.

"Shingan ga aru" (心願がある)– "I have taken a vow."

Shinjin (信心)– "a pious heart", piety.

Shōjin (精進)– fasting.

"Go shōjin desu ka."(御精進ですか)– "Are you fasting?"

Shugyō (修行)– literally, practice stepping up to the doors of strange people while praying aloud, in order to give them the opportunity of showing their charity; often used nowadays as a synonym for begging.

Shugyō ni kakaru (修行に掛かる)– to devote oneself to

shugyō.

Shugyō wo suru (修行をする)– to carry on *shugyō.*

Shirishiki (尻敷)– an apron for sitting on; a piece of cloth, or even of leather, that serves as a seat.

Shirisuke (shirizuke) (尻すけ)– the same as the above.

Takuhachi wo suru (托鉢をする)– "to hold out the bowl", meaning to carry on *shugyō.*

Tateishi (立石)– a stone guide-post.

Tekkō (手甲)– cloth mittens to protect the hands.

Tōri (通り), o tōri (お通り), o tōri nasai (お通りなさい)– "Go on!", "Please go on!" (a refusal of a gift by the person approached).

Tosa wa onikuni (土佐は鬼国)– "Tosa is a land of devils."

Tosa wa onna no jigoku (土佐は女の地獄)– "Tosa is Hell for women."

Tsue (杖), o tsue (お杖)– the pilgrim staff.

Tsūya (通夜)– to spend the night in the temple; usually associated with festivals such as *kaichō.*

Tsuyado (通夜堂)– a hall for pilgrims to stay overnight.

Utsu (打つ)– to strike, to hit at, to give up (the ticket); used even for the visit to a temple.

Uchimodori (打戻り)– the place where the pilgrim must go over the same piece of road twice.

Wakishi (脇師)– auxiliary or secondary deities; usually the statues standing on either side of the chief deity.

Waraji, waranji (草鞋)– straw sandals.

Warōzu (草靴)– straw sandals (change in sound from *waragutsu*); straw shoes.

Yakuyoke (厄除け)– "exorcism", practices to exorcise the danger of certain years (of a person's age).

Yakuyoke Daishi (厄除大師)– see Daishi.

Zenkon suru (善根する)– to give shelter to a pilgrim free of charge. "*Mada hayai ga, o shimainasai; zenkon shimasu yo*" (まだ早いが、おしまいなさい、善根しますよ)– "It is still early, but stop for today. I will put you up for the night."

Zenkonyado (善根宿)– places of free lodging.

Zudabukuro (頭陀袋)– a bag to hold received gifts.

C. Two passports

In the following section I give the translation of two passports that are in my possession. The first was given to me through the courtesy of Professor Chokkō Kageura (Matsuyama), and was issued by the mayor of a village in the year 1823. The second was issued by a temple and bears the date 1812. It was put aside for pasting onto a sliding door in the temple in question, bears no stamp, and is therefore apparently a sample written for practice, or one that for some reason or other was not used. Since it shows some interesting variations in the text, we give it here in translation with the other one.

I. Passport

The wife Hisa and the son Genjirō of Iuemon from the village noted below will soon make the round of Shikoku (*Shikoku Henro*) because of a vow. We therefore request that they be allowed to pass the borders of the different provinces without delay, so that they may be assured of shelter at the approach of (or when they are overtaken) by darkness. As for their belief, it can be proved that they have belonged for generations to the Shingon sect, and are parishioners of Suian-ji in the village noted below. Besides this, they are above suspicion in every respect.

The above pass is ratified by

Iyo Province, the Mayor's office in Niiya, Kita District

The Mayor of the village of Niiya

Jūsa(e)mon Tamai

Bunsei 6th year, in March

To the borders of the provinces

To their honors the mayors

II. Passport

Myōbō (Akifusa), Priest in Daion-ji, in the village of Tachibana, Onsen district, Iyo province.

Since the above-named man departs soon on the Shikoku pilgrimage (*Shikoku junpai*), the borders of the various provinces are requested to let him pass without delay. As for his belief, it has been proved that he belongs to the Shingon sect, being an adherent of the temple of the undersigned. We beg that shelter be given him at the approach of darkness. Should he (on the way) become ill and die, we request that he be buried without further communication (perhaps= "counter questions") with us here, according to the custom of the place where he then is.

The above pass is ratified for the purpose of future reference.

Bunkwa 9th year, 5th month, 5th day

(Temple) Daion-ji (Signature and seal are lacking)

To the Officials of the Provinces.

D. Bibliography

a. Biographies.

I. All older biographies are printed in the collection, Zoku Gunsho Ruiju (続群書類従), Part 8, Chapters 206-210. (Reprinted in October 15, 1927)

1. *Kūkai Sōzu Den* (空海僧都伝), by Shinzei (真済), Kōbō Daishi's pupil. Written in 835, but appeared in a modern day Japanese translation in 1911.

2. *Zō Daisōjō Wajō Denki* (贈大僧正和上伝記), by an abbot of Jōkan-ji, in 895.

3. *Daishi Go Gyōjō Shūki* (大師御行状集記), by Kyōhan (経範), "literary grandchild" of Kōbō Daishi of the 8th generation, in 1089.

4. *Kōbō Daishi Go Den* (弘法大師御伝), by Ihō (維寶), a priest of Kongōbu-ji, in 1718.

5. *Kōbō Daishi Gyōkeki* (弘法大師行化記), by Ryūkan (龍肝), a priest of Kongōbu-ji who died according to an old book in 1825.

6. *Kōya Daishi Go Kōden* (弘法大師御広伝), by Shōken (政賢) in 1118, repeatedly copied, reprinted from the copy of the year 1800.

7. *Kōden Ryakkōshō* (弘伝略頌杪), by Dōhan (道範), in 1234, reprinted from the copy of the year 1794.

II. Kōbō Daishi Seiden (弘法大師正伝), by Kōen (高演), in 1834.

III. Kōbō Daishi Gyōjōki (弘法大師行上記), by an unknown author; 12 manuscript rolls with pictures at Tō-ji temple in Kyoto, reprinted in the collection Kokubun Tōhō Bukkyō Sōsho (国文東方仏教叢書) in Tokyo in 1925.

IV. Of those biographies written in recent times, mostly in the form of pamphlets for the edification of pilgrims, I have used the following:

    1. Schiller, Dr. Pfarrer (trans.). Gogaku no Kumo (五嶽の雲), *Mitteilungen der deutschen Geselschaft Natur- und Volkerkunde Ostasiesns.* Vol XI, 4., (1909): 405-439.

    2. Shimura, Shōsuke (此村庄助). *Kōbō Daishi go Ichidaiki* (弘法大師御一代記) , Osaka, 1922.

    3. Miura, Senshō (三浦仙章). *Kōbō Daishi* (弘法大師), with preface by Chokkō Kageura, Matsuyama, 1917.

    4. Kyōjū, Hiroyasu (広安恭寿). *Kōbō Daishi no Go Itoku* (弘法大師の偉徳), Kyoto, 1903.

    5. Hasū, Kanzen (蓮生勧善). *Kōbō Daishi Go Denki* (弘法大師御伝記), Kyoto, 1921 . Despite it only being 104 pages it is a very good book.

    6. Makino, Shinnosuke (牧野信之助). *Kōbō Daishi den no Kenkyū* (弘法大師の研究), Kyoto, 1921.

    In addition to those cited above, the following books and writings were used in preparing the foregoing work (omitting any special mention of dictionaries such as Bukkyō Daijiten and the Encyclopedia Japonica):

    1. Kageura, Chokkō (影浦直孝). *Iyo Shiseiki* (伊予史

跡), Matsuyama, 1924. A very solid and detailed work on the history of Iyo province.[3]

2. *Iyo Futanashū* (伊予二名集)(Futana is the ancient name of Iyo), by an unknown author, reprinted in 1925 (愛媛青年処女協会), under the editorship of Tan Soga. In addition, I had the use of a copy from the Jōkyō era (1684-1688), in the possession of Professor Kageura.

3. Nagata, Hidejirō (永田秀次郎). *Watakushi no Mitaru Kōbō Daishi* (私の見たる弘法大師); a memorial speech delivered in Osaka in 1926, very instructive as to the ideas of a politician who had become governor, and later mayor of Tokyo.

4. Tomita, Kōjun (富田学純). *Mikkyō Hyakuwa* (密教百話), Tokyo, 1925. A concise statement of the secret teachings of Shingon.

5. Tanimoto, Tomeri (谷本富). *Nippon Bunka to Bukkyō* (日本文化と仏教), 3rd edition, Tokyo, 1924.

6. Inamura, Shudō (稲村修道). *Junreika no Shukyō* (巡禮歌の宗教) ,Osaka, 1927. A study of the Buddhist cult of healing (for the laity), based upon the go-eika of the Saikoku road, with an appendix dealing with the origin of the Saikoku pilgrimage, etc.

7. Shōrō, Masamichi (寺石正道). *Tosa Shiseki Jun-yū* (土佐史跡巡遊), Kochi, 1927. Contains descriptions of most of the historical memorials of Tosa province. The author cannot be said to have caught the spirit of the pilgrimage, since his contact with the pilgrims was very limited, and

---

[3] Editor – could not find this book.

278

wholly by chance.

8. Karl, August Reischauer. *Studies in Japanese Buddhism*, New York, 1917.

9. Lloyd, Arthur. Developments of Japanese Buddhism, *Transactions of the Asiatic Society*, Vol. XXII, (Tokyo, 1894): 337-506.

10. Haas, Hans. "Die kontemplativen Schulen des japanischen Buddhismus." *Mitteilungen der deutschen Geselschaft Natur- und Volkerkunde Ostasiesns*, Vol. X, 2, (Tokyo, 1906): 157-223.

11. Haas, Hans. "Annalen des japanischen Buddhismus." *Mitteilungen der deutschen Geselschaft Natur- und Volkerkunde Ostasiesns*, Vol .XI, 3, (Tokyo, 1908):281-388.

12. Lloyd, Arthur. "Kirchenvater und Mahayanismus." *Mitteilungen der deutschen Gesellschaft fur Natur- und Volkerkunde Ostasiens*, Vol.XI, 4. (Tokyo, 1909): 389-404.

13. Gotō, Michio. (後藤道雄). *Meishin to Igaku* (迷信と医学), Kyoto, 1921. Treats in a special section some cases of superstition in connection with the Shikoku temples, but only, in the province of Awa(Tokushima).

14. Tanaka, Kaiō (田中海応). "Honchō Yakushi Nyorai no Shinkō" (本朝薬師如来の信仰), *Mikkyō*, Vol.III, p.1294 ff.[4]

15. Takeda, Toyoshirō (武田豊四郎). "Minkan

_____

[4] Editor – I was not able to find the periodical Mikkyō, but did discover the article in *Bukkyō Shigaku* (仏教史学), July 25, 1913. p.287-293.

Densetsu yori mitaru Shō Kūkai"(民間伝説より見たる聖空海), *Mikkyō*, Vol.III, p.1285.[5]

16. *Shikoku Reijō* (四国霊場), published by the Society for the Protection of Hanta-ji, 1922. Contains in addition to other essays that by Kageura on the determination of the birthplace of Kūkai. Hanta-ji is the 50th temple of the pilgrimage.

17. Hōjō, Nakata. *Kaizō izen ni okeru Kōyasan Bunkashi* (改造以前における高野山文化史). This appeared in 1921 or 1922.[6]

I refrain from citing in detail the more or less prolix accounts published by the individual temples of the pilgrimage concerning their own particular history and significance.

b. Descriptions of the journey.

I. Gonsōjō, Kenmyō (権僧正賢明). *Kūshō Hōshinnō Shikoku Reijō Gojunkōki* (空性法親王四国霊場御巡行記), in the collection, Kokubun Tōhō Bukkyō Sōsho, Kibōbu (国分東方仏教叢書紀行部), Tokyo, 1914.[7]

---

[5] Editor – The only reference found about this article was "Mikkyō Kenkyūkai, 1913". No page numbers.

[6] Editor – I could not find this book.

[7] Editor – This can also be found in *Shikoku Henrokishu* (四国遍路記集) by Iyo-shidankai (伊予史談会), Aoba Tosho, 1981. p.9-20.

II. Shikokuzaru (pseudonym for Kikutarō Kan) (管菊太郎). *Shikoku Junpaiki* (四国巡拝記), Tokyo Niroku Shinbum (東京二六新聞), April to June, 1903.

III. Kanikumo (pseudonym for Shinohara) (篠原). *Shikoku Hachijūhakkasho Dōgyō Futari* (四国八十八ヶ所同行二人), Ehime Shinpō (愛媛新報), Matsuyama, September to November 1926.

IV. Tomita Kōjun (富田学純). *Shikoku Henro* (四国遍路), Tokyo, 1926.

c. Guidebooks.

I. Shinnen, Yuben (真念宥弁). *Shikokudō Shi-nan* (四國道指南), written in 1686, published (in Osaka) in 1688.

II. *Shikoku Henreidō Shi-nan Sōho Daisei* (四國遍禮道指南增補大成), Osaka, 1836.

III. Tokunō, Tsūgi (得熊通義). *Shikoku Meishoki* (四国名所誌: 古蹟遊覧), Matsuyama, 1896.

IV. Miyoshi, Hirota (三好廣太). *Shikoku Henro Dōgyō Futari* (四國遍路同行二人), 18th edition, Osaka, 1925.

V. Mutō, Kyūzan (武藤休山). *Shikoku Reijō Reisan* (四國霊場禮讃), Matsuyama, 1927.

VI. Kadoya, Tsunegorō (門屋常五郎). *Shikoku Reijō Annai* (四國霊場案内), 2nd edition, Matsuyama, 1924.

VII. *Shikoku Reijō Endō Nōgyō Annnaiki* (四國霊場沿農業道案内記), published by the agricultural cooperatives of the four provinces of Shikoku (愛媛県農会), Matsuyama, 1929.

E. Map of Shikoku

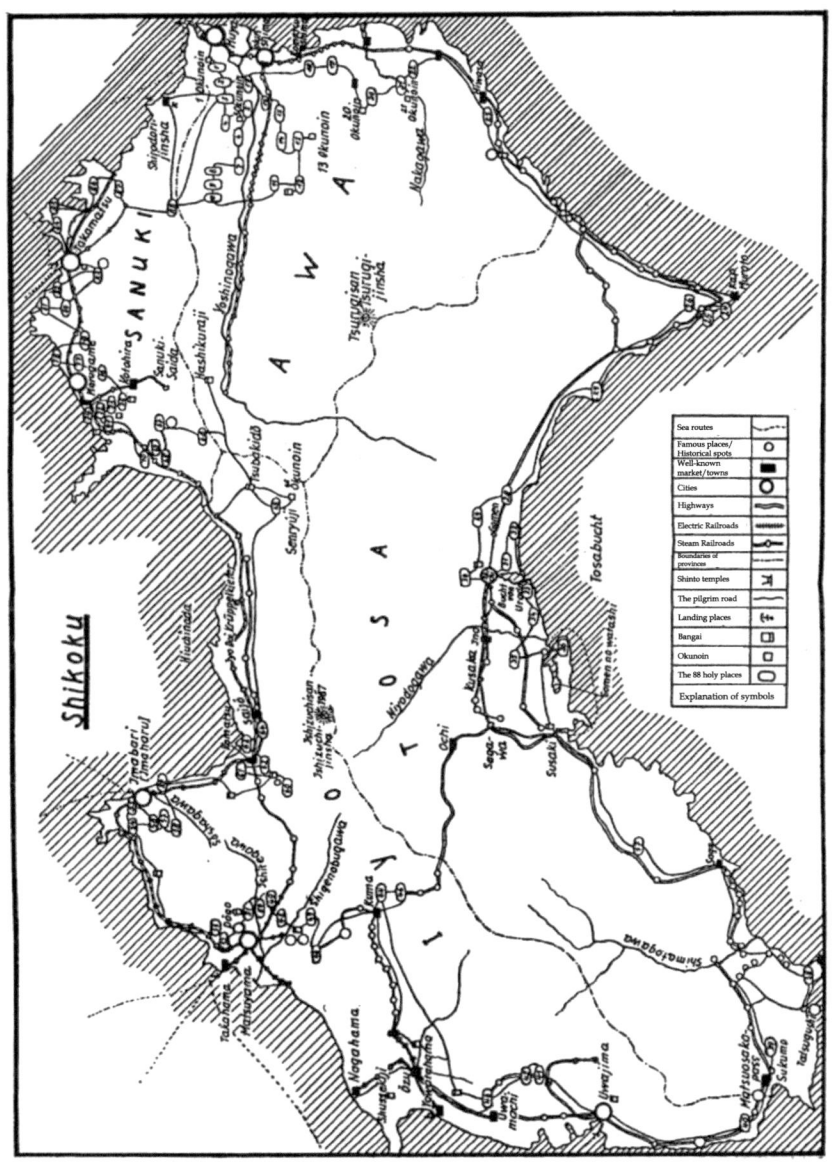

Picture Supplement

1. Temple of Kōbō Daishi's birth. Gate and roofed passage-way.

2. Temple of Kōbō Daishi's birth. View of the temple courtyard.

3. View from the 10th temple looking towards the valley of the Yoshinogawa river.

4. Scene of the Nakagawa river between the 20th and the 21st temples.

5. View of the village of Hiwasa from the 23rd temple.

6. The harbor of Tsuro (Tosa); in the foreground, sharks' fins
hung up to dry, and squids placed on kilns in the sun.

7. The harbor of Tsuro (Tosa), showing the narrow, dangerous way out of a harbor in Tosa.

8. Summer in Tosa; a street scene between the 25th and the 26th temples.

9. The Hondō (Main Hall) of Temple No. 37.

10. The Daishidō of Temple No.28.

11. Tsudera (No.25); general view.

12. The view from Tsudera of Cape Muroto (one of the eight
famous landscapes in Japan).

13. Cormorant fishers with their birds resting at noon in the river-bed of the Niyodo-gawa river.

14. The precipitous coast near the 38th temple.

15. The precipitous coast near the 38th temple.

16. The precipitous coast near the 38th temple.

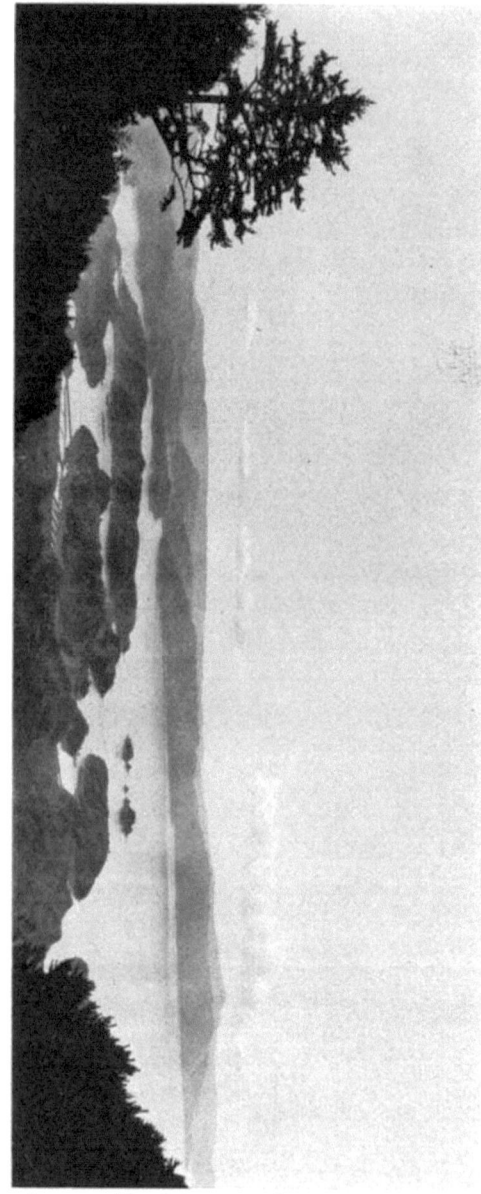

17. Matsuozakatoge (the Matsuozaka Pass); view over the bay of
Sukumo.

18. The riverbed of the Shigenbugawa river, through which the pilgrim road leads between the 47th and the 48th temples.

19. The view from the 58th temple of sunrise over the bay of Hiuchinada in Iyo.

20. On the way to the highest temple of the pilgrimage, where the boundaries of Iyo, Sanuki, and Awa join.

21. The old lighthouse (takatorō) of Kotohira, in Sanuki.

22. A guide-post between the 42ⁿᵈ and the 43ʳᵈ temples.

23. A general view of Temple No. 23.

24. A general view of Temple No. 15.

25. A general view of Temple No. 11.

26. The Niōmon at Temple No. 1.

27. The Niōmon at Temple No. 70.

28. The Niōmon at Temple No. 65.

29. An old woman selling cakes in the Niōmon of Temple No. 40.

30. The view from the Niōmon into the temple courtyard at Temple No. 86.

31. At Temple No. 58, a view of the Hondō, with the roofed passage-way to the Daishi-dō, and in the right foreground the stone wash-basin.

32. At Temple No. 27 the wash-basin, where, instead of the dragon, a bamboo pipe spews forth water, and a hand-towel is hung on a small branch of bamboo at the left.

33. At Temple No. 38, the Hondō, built in a flat style, and under Imperial protection.

34. At Temple No.34, a building dating from the Genroku Era
(1688-1704).

35. At Temple No.43, a side-view of the building dating from the
Genroku Era, with a gable of the present-day Hondō in the
background.

36. At Temple No.1, the Hondō, with a high roof in the style of the Tokugawa Era.

37. At Temple No.4, the Hondō, in the form that appears most often.

38. At Temple No.13, the Hondō, showing a break in the lower line of the roof, and beautiful proportions.

39. At Temple No.46, the Hondō, showing the growth of the front door.

40. At Temple No.43, the Hondō, showing the more pronounced
growth of the front roof, and many votive pictures.

41. At Temple No.21, the Hondō, showing the growth of the front
gable.

42. At Temple No.75, the Okunoin (temple of the Daishi's birth), the Hondō, showing an increase in the size of the front gable.

43. At Temple No.88, the Hondō, showing a gable almost as high as the ridge-pole.

44. At Temple No.87, Hondō and Pagoda, showing a gable that is as high as the ridge-pole.

45. At Temple No.15, a two-storied Hondō.

46. At Temple No. 21, the Daishidō.

47. At Temple No.27, the bell-tower, open form.

308

48. At Temple No.60, the bell-tower, open form.

49. At Temple No.51, the bell-tower, closed form (under Imperial protection).

50. At Temple No.51, the three-storied pagoda with the two-storied Niōmon, both under Imperial protection.

51. At Temple No.70, the five-storied pagoda.

310

52. At Temple No.8, the treasure pagoda.

53. At Temple No.2, a small stone pagoda and statues of Buddha.

54. At Temple No.17, the Kyōzō (sutra storehouse).

55. At Temple No.67, a roofed passage-way and a statue of Jizō.

56. At Temple No.19, the cemetery.

57. At Temple No.79, a Shinto-shrine gate of very beautiful construction at the entrance, and, behind it, the principal building of the Buddhist temple.

58. At Temple No.12, a view of the Daishidō and the Hondō through the Shinto-shrine gate.

59. At Temple No.41, a second Shinto-shrine gate, standing between the Daishidō and the Hondō.

60. At Temple No.60, the Hondō, built in the style of a Shinto shrine.

61. Statues of the Daishi and of Emon Saburō made of pilgrims' tickets.

62. Two pilgrims from Hok-kaidō in front of a shop with straw sandals; beside the sandals hangs a piece of hollow bamboo on which the price (5 sen) is written; the pilgrims takes the sandals and place the money for them in the hollow bamboo. In earlier times such shops were found everywhere, dealing in other wares as well; and even today they are still found in many places in the mountains.

63. A mother with her daughters on the pilgrimage. They are not making the pilgrimage in white garments, but in all other respects they are equipped according to instructions given to pilgrims.

316

64. Three pilgrims (two men and one woman) of the Jōkyō Era (1684-1687), in an illustration from Shikokudō Shi-nan.

65. The same picture from the guidebook of the Bunkwa Era (1804-1817). The foremost pilgrim appears to be a priest.

66. A wayside shrine between the 64th and the 65th temples hung with pilgrims' tickets.

67. A portion of the Daishidō of the 26th temple.

68. The Nōkyōsho of Temple No.9.

69. Gomen no Watashi; Inoshiri in the neighbourhood of the 36th temple is in the right foreground, and Usa is opposite it.

70. A leper at Ishite temple (No.51).

71. At Temple No.66, the Tsūyado (3900 ft. above sea-level).

72. Pilgrims spending the night in the open.

73. The Daishidō of the 43rd temple, with facsimiles of women's breasts made of cloth.

74. The Daishidō of the 44ᵗʰ temple, with a cripple's cart at the right and at the left, and a plaster cast beside the right joist of the front roof.

75. At Temple No.51, a portion of the Niōmon, with a view of the pagoda.

76. At Temple No87, the Niōmon, with straw sandals as long as a man is tall.

77. A statue of Binzuru at the 54th temple, with several sacred shrines in the background.

78. The Gyūōdō at Temple No.42.

79. A guidepost to the 88th temple, with the inscription
"Ketsugwansho" (Place of Fulfillment of the vow).

Three pages from a "Written Offering Book" (one-half original size)

80a. Temple No. 60; clear writing, large seals
1st line – Kyō wa osametate-matsuru
2nd line – Siddhami-sign "vam" (Japanese: ban), Dainichi Nyorai.
3rd line – Iyo Yokomine-ji.Abb.
80a: Tempel 60..

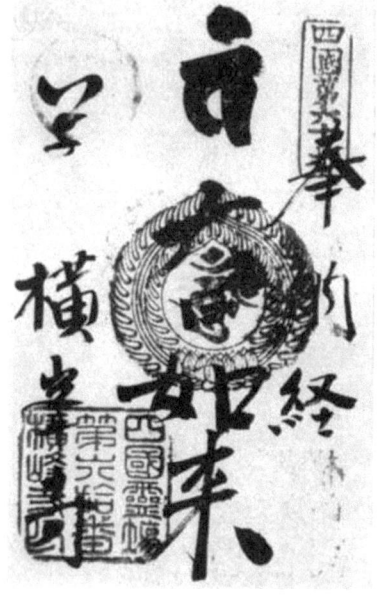

80b. Temple No.41; written by a ten-year-old boy.
1st line – Hōnō (osametate-matsuru)
2nd line – Jūichimen Kanseon.
3rd line – Inariyama.Abb.

80c. Temple No.42; very distinct writing full of character, small seals.

1st line – Hōnō (osametatematsuru)
2nd line – Honson Dainichi Nyorai
3rd line – Butsumoku-ji.

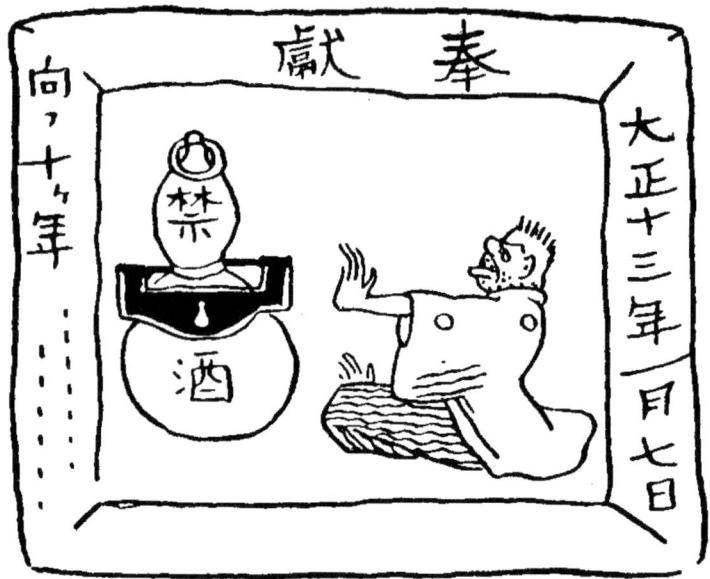

81. A Votive Picture form the Konpira Shrine at Kotohira (from the travel periodical "Setonaikai", March, 1924, p47)
Inscription:
Above horizontal (reading right to left): "Hōken" (Humbly offered)
Right: "Taishō 13 nen 1gatsu nanuka" (January 7, 1924).
Left: "Mukō jukkanen" (For the next ten years)
Below: (Name of man making the offering discreetly omitted)
Picture: A man making a gesture of refusal sits before a drinking gourd about which a large lock is hung and on which are written the two characters, "Kinshū" (Wine forbidden). The character kin (forbidden) is written so that it becomes the severely forbidding face of the drinking-gourd.

Explanation: The Konpira Shrine, which does not to be sure belong to the pilgrimage, but which is visited by most of the pilgrims, is the shrine of seafaring men. To become seasick is called in Japanese, *fune in yō* (to become drunk from (riding on) a ship).

Many people therefore take a vow here not to get drunk with wine anymore in the future, in the hope that they will likewise by the mercy of Konpira get drunk no more from (riding on) a ship.

Two tickets of pilgrims from Tokyo

82. The ticket of a pilgrim by the name of Takatsuki, who is making the pilgrimage for the 12th time, as noted above in handwriting. The character in the circle, kyō, is red; otherwise, the ticket is black and white. (Three-quarters original size)

83. The ticket of a society from Tokyo, the Kōseikō, with the names and the addresses of the members making the pilgrimage. In the middle there are the characters Hōnō (I offer or We offer), a facsimile of the trident, the characters Na-mu Daishi Henjō Kongō, the name of the society, and the name of its founder. The border is black and lilac, and in four places the writing is red. (Three-quarters original size)

84. The ticket of a Mr. Hamamura of Kyoto, the kana syllables ha ma mu ra forming the contours of his face. (One half original size)

Genuine Pilgrims' tickets from Shikoku

85a. A ticket written entirely by hand, showing the prescribed proportions. Wishes in the form of prayers such as "Great Peace Under Heaven" are lacking. A red swastika is printed in the middle. (One-half original size).

85b. A ticket with a prefix, without a picture of the Daishi. Instead of a wish in the form of a prayer, there is "Namu Daishi Henjō Kongō" on the right side, and under it "Dōgyō Futari." (Two-thirds original size)

85c. A ticket with a prefix and a picture of the Daishi. Above to the right and to the left are the wishes: "Great Peace Under Heaven" and "Increase of the Five Grains", and to the right of the middle, "Peace and Security for the Family." (Two-thirds original size).

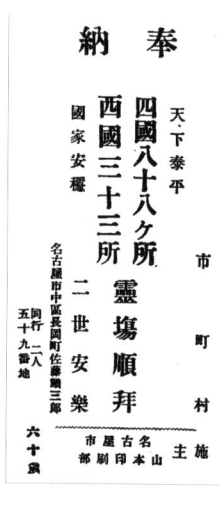

85d. A ticket printed from a specially-made woodblock for a 70-year-old man, who is making the pilgrimage for himself and his late wife and who therefore writes, "Dōgyō Sannin" (Three on a pilgrimage) instead of the usual "Two." (Somewhat reduced in size)

85e. The red ticket of a pilgrim who has made the pilgrimage more than seven times. (Two-thirds original size)

85f. The green ticket of a pilgrim who is combining the Shikoku pilgrimage with the Saikoku pilgrimage. At the bottom of the ticket stand the words: "Seshu: Nagoya Shi Yamamoto Insatsubu." The tickets are therefore presented as settai by the Yamamoto Printing Establishment in Nagoya. I have found a similar mark on other tickets. (Two-thirds original size)

86. A likeness of Kōbō Daishi and above it Dainichi Nyorai. (Taken from a woodblock in the possession of my brother in Osaka)

87. A charm of Butsumoku-ji, printed from a woodblock dating from the Genroku Era. (For a description, see p. 229). The charm is as large as a sheet of *hanshi*. (One-half original size)

石鉄山

88. A charm of Yokomine-ji. (For a description, see p. 231)
(Three-quarters original size).